# Passport t

## The Tourist's Guide ~~to Pub Etiquette~~

## Kate Fox

Brewers and Licensed Retailers Association

First Published 1996
Brewers and Licensed Retailers Association
42 Portman Square, London W1H 0BB

In association with

The Do-Not Press
PO Box 4215, London SE23 2QD

A CIP catalogue record for this book
is available from the British Library

ISBN 1–899344–09–8

Printed and bound in the UK

# Contents

# Introduction

**Q. *Why should I go to pubs?***

**A.** By all means visit Stonehenge and Buckingham Palace, but if you want to see what real life in Britain is all about, you have to go to the pub. Pub-going is by far the most popular native pastime. The 61,000 pubs in Britain have over 25 million loyal customers. Over three-quarters of the adult population go to pubs, and over a third are 'regulars', visiting the pub at least once a week. The pub is a central part of British life and culture. If you haven't been to a pub, you haven't seen Britain.

Visitors to Britain are bewitched by our pubs, but they are often bothered and bewildered by the unwritten rules of pub etiquette. This is not surprising: the variety and complexity of pub customs and rituals can be equally daunting for inexperienced British pubgoers.

Even at the very simplest level, ignorance of the rules can cause problems – such as unsatisfied thirst. Gasping for a beer, the innocent tourists go into a pub, sit down and wait for someone to serve them… (see Chapter 1). The more complex aspects of pub etiquette – the intricate behaviour-codes governing every moment from "what's yours?" to "time, ladies and gentlemen" – are an infinite source of misunderstanding, confusion and potential embarrassment.

Experienced native pubgoers obey the unspoken rules, but without being conscious of doing so. Regulars will mutter and grumble when an uninitiated tourist commits a breach of pub etiquette, but may well be unable to tell him exactly what rule he has broken. Just as native speakers can rarely explain the grammatical rules of their own language, those who are most fluent in particular rituals, customs and traditions generally lack the detachment necessary to explain the 'grammar' of these practices in an intelligible manner. This is why we have anthropologists.

Most anthropologists go off to remote parts of the world to live among exotic tribes, observe their behaviour and ask endless questions in order to understand and explain their strange customs. In 1992, the BLRA asked the experienced social scientists at MCM Research to apply the same research techniques in the British pub. Some of MCM's findings were published in *Pubwatching with Desmond Morris* (1993) and its sequel *Women in Pubs* (1994). In 1995, for *Passport to the Pub*, the MCM Research team – led by Research Manager Joe McCann and Senior Researcher John Middleton – embarked on yet another six-month anthropological pub-crawl. In total, the research on which this book is based has involved observation work in over 800 pubs, consultations with over 500 publicans and bar staff and interviews with over 1000 pubgoers – both natives and tourists.

Our first task in the preliminary research for this project was to find out how much tourists knew about pub etiquette. Not surprisingly, given the lack of information available, we found that what tourists *didn't* know about pub etiquette would fill a book. This is the book.

# The Basics

**Q:** *What is a pub?*

**A:** 'Pub' is short for 'Public House'. The publican opens part of his or her 'house' to the public – a bit like giving a party in your own home every day! This is why the publican is often called the 'host'. The home-like qualities of the British pub are perhaps why tourists often find our pubs more cosy and welcoming than bars and cafes in other parts of the world.

**Q:** *How do I know it's a pub?*

**A:** This is not a silly question. In other parts of the world, cafes and bars often display the words 'cafe' or 'bar' in a prominent position on the facade or signage. You will rarely see the word 'pub' anywhere on a British pub, and our traditional curtains and frosted windows mean you cannot see much from the outside, so how can the uninitiated first-time visitor tell that he or she is looking at a pub, rather than a restaurant, coffee shop or night-club? There is one important external feature which can tell you that it is a pub: the pub-sign. The pub-sign is mounted about 15 to 25 feet from the ground, either sticking out at right-angles to the building or swinging in a wooden frame at the top of a pole outside the building. The sign usually measures about 3 by 4 feet, and displays both the name of the pub and a pictorial representation of the name. For example, a pub called The White Horse will have a sign showing the name and a picture of a white horse. The name of the pub will usually be repeated in large letters on the front of the building itself.

## Getting served

**Official rules:** By law, pubs are not allowed to open until 11am (noon on Sundays). They cannot serve drinks after 11pm (10.30 on Sundays) – although you are allowed 20 minutes to finish any drinks already purchased. In Scotland pubs generally open until midnight. Do not even try to get served outside these legal 'licensing hours'. It is also illegal for pubs to serve alcoholic drinks to anyone under the age of

18, and you will be breaking the law if you try to buy an alcoholic drink for anyone who is under 18.

So much for the official rules and regulations. The unofficial, unwritten, unspoken rules of pub etiquette are far more complex – but just as important.

☞ **Rule number one**: There is no waiter service in British pubs. You have to go up to the bar to buy your drinks, and carry them back to your table.

One of the saddest sights of the British summer (or the funniest, depending on your sense of humour) is the group of thirsty tourists sitting at a table in a pub, patiently waiting for someone to come and take their order. In most cases, a friendly native will put them out of their misery by explaining rule number one, or they will figure it out for themselves, but in a busy pub it can be some time before the correct procedure becomes clear.

 **Regional variation:** You may find waiter service in some pubs in Northern Ireland, but not all. Even there, waiter service is not common in city-centre pubs, and some pubs only use waiters at very busy times. Where waiter service is available, it is a supplement to bar service, not a replacement. So, when in doubt, use the bar.

## Social benefits

Once they are aware of the no-waiter-service rule in British pubs, most tourists recognise it as an advantage, rather than an inconvenience. Having to go up to the bar for your drinks ensures plenty of opportunities for social contact between customers.

In bars and cafes in other parts of the world, waiter service can isolate people at separate tables, which makes it more difficult to initiate contact with others. Perhaps many cultures are more naturally outgoing and sociable than the British, and do not require any assistance in striking up a conversation with those seated near them.

**Research findings:** In observation-studies, we timed first-time tourists to find out exactly how long it would take them to discover the no-waiter-service rule. The fastest time – just under two-and-a-half minutes – was achieved by a sharp-eyed American couple. The slowest – over 45 minutes – involved a group of six young Italians. This group did not, however, seem particularly concerned about the apparent lack of service, being engrossed in a lively debate about football. Sympathy should go to the French couple who marched out of the pub, complaining bitterly to each other about the poor service and British manners in general, after a 24-minute wait.

The British, however, are a somewhat reserved and inhibited people, and we need all the help we can get! It is much easier to drift casually into a spontaneous chat while waiting at the bar than deliberately to break into the conversation at another table. Like every other aspect of pub etiquette, the no-waiter-service system is designed to promote sociability.

This is very good news for tourists who wish to make contact with the natives. The bar counter in a pub is possibly the only site in the British Isles in which friendly conversation with strangers is considered entirely appropriate and normal behaviour.

**Note:** In Britain, the term 'bar' can mean either the actual counter at which drinks are served, or any room in the pub which contains one of these counters. You may come across pubs with rooms marked 'Public Bar' and 'Lounge Bar' or 'Saloon Bar'. The Public Bar usually has more modest and functional furnishings, and houses pub-games such as pool and darts, while the Lounge or Saloon Bar is more luxurious, comfortable and conducive to quiet conversation. Traditionally, both prices and social classes were lower in the Public Bar, but these distinctions no longer apply.

**Rule number two**: It is customary for one or two people, not the whole group, to go up to the bar to buy drinks.

Bar staff are generally very tolerant people, but large packs of tourists crowding the bar counter can try their patience. It is best if only one or at the most two members of the group approach the bar to purchase drinks for the group. Other members of the group should either stand back from the bar or go and sit down at a table.

Before you can order at all, you must learn the correct bar-counter etiquette. You will notice that the bar counter of the pub is the only place in Britain in which anything is sold or served without the formation of a queue. Many visitors have observed that queuing is almost a national pastime for the British, who will automatically arrange themselves into an orderly line at bus stops, shop counters, ice-cream stalls, lifts, entrances, exits – and sometimes in the middle of nowhere for no apparent reason.

In the pub, by contrast, we gather haphazardly along the bar counter. This may appear contrary to all native instincts and customs, until you realise – and this is spooky – that the queue is still there, and the bar staff are aware of each person's position in the 'invisible' queue.

Bar staff are remarkably skilled at identifying who is next in the invisible queue at the counter, but they are not infallible. You need to attract their attention to make them aware that you are waiting to be served.

## The pantomime ritual

☞ **Rule number three:** To get served, you must attract the attention of the bar staff without making any noise or resorting to the vulgarity of too-obvious gesticulation. This is much easier than it sounds!

There are strict rules of etiquette involved in attracting the attention of bar staff. The ritual procedure is best described as a sort of subtle pantomime – not the kind of children's pantomime you see on stage at Christmas, more like an Ingmar Bergman film in which the twitch of an eyebrow speaks volumes.

The object is to catch the barman's eye. Eye contact is all that is necessary to ensure that you have been spotted and will be served in your turn. The following do's and don'ts will help you to achieve this without breaching the unwritten laws of pub etiquette and incurring the disapproval of the natives.

⊠ **Don't** ever try to 'jump' the invisible queue. The people who reached the bar before you will be served before you. Everyone is well aware of his or her place in the queue, and any obvious attempt to get served out of turn will be ignored by bar staff and frowned upon by other customers.

☑ **Do** start by trying to identify the best position at the bar counter. When the bar is busy, there are two positions which may be favourable for making eye-contact with bar staff. One is immediately opposite the till, as bar staff must return there after each sale. Skilled bar staff, however, are aware of the 'till-position-manoeuvre' and may have perfected gaze-avoidance techniques to prevent customers who adopt this strategy from jumping the queue. A more potentially effective strategy is to position yourself next to a person currently being served, as bar staff will find it hard to avoid eye-contact with you when they hand over drinks and take money from your immediate neighbour.

⊠ **Don't** call out to the bar staff, tap coins on the counter, snap your fingers, wave like a drowning swimmer, bang your hand on the counter, shout "service" or "barman" or wave money about. In fact, it is best to avoid all speech or obvious gesticulation.

☑ **Do** let the bar staff know you are waiting to be served by holding money or your empty glass in your hand. You may tilt the empty glass, perhaps even turn it slowly in a circular motion (some say that this indicates the passing of time). If the wait continues, you may perch your elbow on the bar, with either money or empty glass in your raised hand – but never raise your whole arm and wave the notes or glass around.

☒ **Don't** scowl, frown or glare at the bar staff, or make your impatience obvious by heavy sighing and angry muttering. The bar staff are doing their best to serve everyone in turn, and rudeness will not help your cause.

☑ **Do** adopt an expectant, hopeful, even slightly anxious facial expression. If you look too contented and complacent, the bar staff may assume you are already being served.

☒ **Don't** ring the bell. Some pubs have a large bell attached to the wall at one end of the bar. This is used by the publican or bar staff to signal 'last orders' and 'time' (see Chapter 5 for explanation). If you ring the bell, customers may interpret this as the 'last orders' signal, and will all rush to the bar to buy their last drinks - making it even more difficult for you to get served, and incurring the wrath of the publican!

☑ **Do** stay alert and keep your eye on the bar staff at all times. This will increase your chances of making eye-contact.

✋ **Exceptions:** If you hear people calling out "Get a move on!" or "I've been stood here since last Thursday!" or "Any chance of a drink sometime this week?" to the bar staff, do *not* imitate them. The only people permitted to make such remarks are established regulars, and the remarks are made in the context of the special etiquette governing relations between bar staff and regulars. (See Chapter 3, *Making Contact,* for tips on how to spot regulars and Chapter 9, *Going Native,* for further details of the privileges enjoyed by regulars.)

When you achieve your goal of making eye contact with the barman, a quick lift of the eyebrows and upwards jerk of the chin, accompanied by a hopeful smile, will let him know that you are waiting. In a busy bar, do not expect a verbal response. Bar staff will respond to your non-verbal signals with a smile or a nod, a raised finger or hand, perhaps accompanied by a similar eyebrow-lift. This conveys that they have seen you waiting and will serve you as soon as possible.

Natives perform the pantomime instinctively, without being aware that they are following a rigid etiquette, and without ever questioning the extraordinary handicaps – no speaking, no waving, no noise, constant alertness to subtle non-verbal signals, etc. – imposed by this etiquette.

**Research findings:** If you find this ritual baffling, you are not alone: most of the tourists we interviewed found it utterly incredible. A Dutch visitor expressed the views of many when he said: *"I cannot understand how the British ever manage to buy themselves a drink".*

In fact, the pantomime ritual is much less difficult than it sounds, and you will soon get used to it. After only a few pub-visits, you will realise that good bar staff are exceptionally acute readers of body language, sensitive to very small signals in the posture and expression of their customers. You will see that there is no need to shout and wave at these expert observers, who ensure that everyone does get served, usually in the right order, and without undue fuss, noise or loss of temper.

## Ordering etiquette

☞ **Rule number four**: If you wish to pay for your drinks individually, then order individually; if you order as a group, the bar staff will total the cost and expect a single payment.

A common sight during the tourist season is the large group of tourists monopolising the entire bar counter, trying to order drinks collectively and pay individually, confusing the bar staff and annoying the regulars. If the bar is busy, individual orders and payments will waste your time and the bar staffs', so it is best to elect a 'spokesperson' to order and pay for the drinks.

☞ **Rule number five**: In most British pubs, you pay for your drinks in cash, immediately when you order them.

In terms of financial transactions, the ordinary British local is not a 20th-century business. Although you will find some exceptions, the majority of local pubs do not take credit cards for drinks, and you will have to ask if you want a receipt. You should also expect to pay for each drink or round of drinks when you order it. Credit cards are becoming more widely accepted when ordering meals, but ask before relying on them.

## Ordering beer: the basics

Simply asking for "a beer" in a British pub is a bit like asking for "a wine" in a French restaurant. There are hundreds of different varieties of beer available, each with its own distinctive taste and characteristics. Pubs often have a range of around 20 different beers behind the bar, many of them on draught (on tap), some in bottles and a few in cans. They range from dark stouts, through mild ales and bitter to lager – a light, gold-coloured beer. (You would normally get lager if you just asked for a beer in most other countries, including Europe, the United States and Australia.) In Scotland, bitter is described as 'heavy' or '70/-' (Seventy Shilling Ale).

Don't worry – you don't have to become a connoisseur to enjoy British beer. At a basic level, the bar staff just need to know whether you want bitter, lager or another sort of beer, and whether you want a pint, a half, or one of the wide variety of imported and domestic beers sold by the bottle (look at the glass-fronted coolers and shelves behind the bar to see what bottled beers are available).

A pint is 0.568 litres (i.e. quite a big drink). 'A half' means a half-pint. The 'pint' element is silent. When ordering, you just say *"A half of lager, please"* or *"A half of bitter, please"*. This is very often shortened to *"Half a lager, please"* and so on. The 'please' is important.

If you are interested, there is a lot more to find out about the endless different varieties of traditional British beers. Some publicans and bar staff are very knowledgeable, and will be happy – when they are not too busy serving the stuff – to explain it all to you. Some natives are also extremely well-informed on this subject, and will probably tell you much more than you could ever wish to know about the merits of different beers.

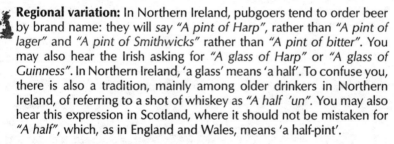

**Regional variation:** In Northern Ireland, pubgoers tend to order beer by brand name: they will *say "A pint of Harp"*, rather than *"A pint of lager"* and *"A pint of Smithwicks"* rather than *"A pint of bitter"*. You may also hear the Irish asking for *"A glass of Harp"* or *"A glass of Guinness"*. In Northern Ireland, 'a glass' means 'a half'. To confuse you, there is also a tradition, mainly among older drinkers in Northern Ireland, of referring to a shot of whiskey as *"A half 'un"*. You may also hear this expression in Scotland, where it should not be mistaken for *"A half"*, which, as in England and Wales, means 'a half-pint'.

## The *"And one for yourself"* ritual

☞ **Rule number six:** It is not customary to tip the publican or bar staff in British pubs. Instead, if you wish, the common practice is to buy them a drink.

To understand this particular element of pub etiquette, you need to understand both the British attitude towards money, and the social structure of the pub. The British tend to be rather squeamish and embarrassed about money. Any sign of excessive interest in money is considered vulgar, and obvious displays of wealth are viewed with contempt rather than admiration. The publican and bar staff may be providing you with a service in exchange for money, but it is not appropriate to emphasise this aspect of

**Research findings:** American visitors experienced particular language-barrier problems with two drinks: cider and Martini. Please note that cider, in Britain, is an alcoholic drink, of about the same strength as beer. If you order *"A Martini"*, you will not get a cocktail: you will get a glass of Martini (vermouth) – no gin or vodka, and no olive.

the relationship. The social structure of the pub is egalitarian: those serving behind the bar are in no way inferior to the customers – indeed, the publican often commands great respect. To give them a tip would be a reminder of their 'service' role, whereas to offer a drink is to treat them as equals.

Buying the person who serves you a drink is not quite the equivalent of giving a tip – it is by no means automatic or expected, in the way tips are more or less automatic in many countries. Offering a drink is a genuinely personal and friendly gesture.

The correct etiquette for offering a drink to the publican or bar staff is to say *"and one for yourself?"*, or *"and will you have one yourself?"* at the end of your order. (If you are not ordering drinks at the time, you may ask *"Will you have a drink?"*, but the first procedure is better, as it implies that you are having a drink together.) Make your offer a question, not an instruction, and do not bellow it out as though determined that the entire pub should be aware of your generosity. If you want to be impeccably British about it, avoid using the word 'buy'. To say *"Can I buy you a drink?"* is acceptable, but

---

**Some bar staff's pet hates:**

❶ *"People who keep everyone waiting while they decide what they want to drink."*

❷ *"People who can't remember their order, and have to keep running back and forth or shouting over to their friends."*

❸ *"People who order the Guinness last."* (Guinness and other stouts such as Beamish, Murphy's and Gillespie's take a while to pour and settle. Always order these drinks first, so that the bar staff can allow them to settle while preparing the rest of the round.)

❹ *"People who try to get rid of their old coins when I've got a queue of customers waiting."* (Counting out pennies causes delay and will annoy waiting customers as well as busy bar staff.)

❺ *"People who hog the bar counter when the pub is very busy, blocking the way so other people can't get served."* (By all means stand or sit at the bar when the pub is relatively quiet, as this is the best way to meet people – see Chapter 3, Making Contact – but move away from the counter when the bar is crowded.)

❻ *"Tourists who come in the pub just to use the toilets – someone should tell them the difference between a Public House and a Public Convenience!"* ('Public Convenience' is the British euphemism for public toilets. Toilets in pubs are for the use of customers, not the general public. Speaking of euphemisms, toilets in pubs are called 'The Ladies' or 'The Gents' and the signs on the toilet doors say 'Ladies' and 'Gentlemen'.)

it does suggest that money is involved. The natives are quite aware that money is involved, but prefer not to draw attention to the fact.

If your *"and one for yourself"* offer is accepted, the publican or bar staff will say *"Thank you, I'll have a half* (or whatever)" and add the price of their chosen drink to the total cost of your order. They will state the new total clearly – *"That'll be four pounds twenty then, please"*. In this way, they can let you know the price of the drink you have just bought them, without directly mentioning the amount. The amount will not be large, as etiquette requires publicans and bar staff to chose a relatively inexpensive beverage when a customer offers them a drink. By stating the revised total, they are also, in an indirect fashion, making you aware of their abstemious choice.

This may initially seem like an unnecessarily convoluted and tortuous way of giving someone a tip. Most visitors, however, find the *"and one for yourself"* ritual a refreshingly friendly alternative to the impersonal handing over of coins.

Feel free to offer a drink even when the bar is busy and the publican or member of staff will not have time to consume it immediately, or even to join you at all. It is quite appropriate for them to accept your offer, add the price of their drink to your order, and enjoy it later when the bar is less crowded. On pouring the drink, even several hours later, the recipient will try to catch your eye, and raise the glass to you in acknowledgement with a nod and a smile, perhaps saying *"cheers"* or *"thanks"* if you are within earshot.

## Ordering food

There is no single, correct way to order a meal or snack in a pub. Different pubs have different systems for ordering food: some take meal orders at the bar, others have separate counters for food. Some pubs have menus on the tables, others have menus on the bar counter or chalked on blackboards – or both.

**Tourist mistake:** A Japanese couple looked at the 'bar snacks menu' and ordered five dishes each, thinking that a 'bar snack' must be the British equivalent of a tiny sushi-bar portion. In British pubs, a bar snack is a simple, one-item meal – such as a sandwich, a hamburger, a pizza, a pork pie, etc. – but it is still a meal, not a nibble! In a small, quiet pub, the bar staff would have realised that the order must be a mistake, but this unfortunate couple happened to be in a very large, busy pub, where the staff assumed that they were ordering for a group of ten.

Wherever and however food is served, drinks must almost always be purchased at the bar, so the best strategy is to go up to the bar first, order your drinks and ask the bar staff what the procedure is for ordering food.

Even if your food is brought to you at your table, the no-waiter-service rule will probably still apply to drinks, so do not expect the staff who bring your food to take orders for drinks as well. You may find this custom irritating, but try to appreciate the opportunities it gives you for friendly chats with the bar staff and other natives. Pubs are not just about food and drink: pubs are about sociability, and every trip to the bar to buy drinks is another chance to make contact.

# 2

# *Choosing Your Pub*

Now that you know the basics, you can be confident about going into any pub in Britain. Your only problem is the sheer number and variety of pubs to choose from.

☞ **Rule number one**: There is no such thing as a typical British pub

If you ask a native to show you a typical British pub, he or she might well take you to the nearest 'pretty-postcard-traditional' pub – one that looks like the pubs in the glossy tourist brochures – because we think this will match your expectations. It may well be a very pleasant, friendly pub, and, if you are lucky, it might not be full of other tourists. It may be a fine example of a truly British pub, but it will not be the *whole* truth.

The truth is that the typical British pub does not exist, or, if you prefer, that there are at least 61,000 typical British pubs. There are over 61,000 pubs in Britain. They are all different. They are all typical. This should not be a problem for the tourist. This is good news. It means that whatever your tastes and preferences, however fussy or eccentric you may be, you can find a pub to suit you.

☞ **Rule number two**: If you know where to look, and what to look for, you can find your ideal pub.

Do not expect different types of pub to be conveniently labelled – we identify them through subtle clues in the decor, the appearance and behaviour of customers, the style of service, the music, the types of drinks and pub-games on display.

**Research findings:** Most of the tourists we interviewed were keen to find a 'typical British pub'. American tourists were particularly obsessed with this question of authenticity, wanting to be constantly reassured that the pub they were in, the beer, the food – and even the barman – were 'typically British'. Bar staff, generally a tolerant breed, found these persistent enquiries amusing, sometimes even endearing. Being anxious to please the customer, they almost invariably answered "oh yes, very typical".

Here are a few common types of pub, with tips on where to find them, how to identify them and what to expect.

## The Local

Natives will often refer to a particular pub as "my local". This is not necessarily the pub nearest to their home, but rather their favourite among a choice of pubs within their community.

### Where to look

Any primarily residential area – whether town-centre, suburb or village (the housing-estate pub is a special, highly distinctive type of local which is covered separately below). You will not find many locals on the main tourist track. Wander away from the big tourist attractions and main shopping centres, towards the back-streets and suburbs – places where people actually live. Here you will find the local pubs on street corners, or sometimes in the middle of a row of ordinary houses.

### When to visit

Evenings and weekends. If the pub is in a purely residential area, it may be rather 'dead' and empty during the working day, only coming to life in the evening and at weekends. If you want a comfortable chat with the publican or bar staff, go along a bit earlier in the day, when they will be less busy serving other customers.

### What to look for

External clues  Although some locals are as ancient and historically interesting as the more famous pubs on the tourist-track, they tend not to advertise their history so blatantly. You are unlikely to see any 'Ye Olde 17th-Century Inn' signs in the ordinary residential streets and suburbs. Even some very picturesque village locals are remarkably modest about their heritage status. The facade of a local will usually be simple and unpretentious

**Research findings:** The majority of tourists we interviewed were unaware of the variety and choice of pub types and styles available. In particular, young tourists visiting 'tourist-traditional' pubs said they would prefer a livelier atmosphere, but were not aware of the existence of 'circuit' pubs, 'student' pubs and other lively, youth-oriented pubs. Also, many parents with young children did not know about the children's facilities and entertainment available at the larger 'family' pubs. Many tourists of all ages were keen to venture off the tourist-track and visit 'ordinary' pubs, but had no idea of where to look, what to look for, or how to behave when they got there!

**Tourist Mistake:** A village publican running a particularly pleasant pub called The Red Lion was told by an American tourist that his pub was *"much nicer than the other pubs I have visited in the 'Red Lion' chain"*. Please do not mistake common pub-names for branded chains. You will find a White Horse, a Red Lion, a King's Arms, a Rose & Crown etc. in almost every town. These are not chains: they are individual, unconnected pubs which happen to have very popular names.

– just the pub-sign and the name on the front of the building. At most, there may be a few signs in the windows to inform you that food, games or satellite TV sports are available. You may see the occasional poster, banner or board advertising forthcoming or regular events such as live music or a pub quiz.

Size and layout
Locals come in all shapes and sizes. The average town-centre local is likely to be quite small, although it may well have the traditional two-room layout, with a 'public bar' and a 'lounge bar'. Suburban locals are generally much more spacious, and 'estate' locals (see below) can be enormous.

Decor
Again, there is wide variation. But if you have only visited the historic pubs in your tourist guidebook – with carefully-tended fireplaces, beams, horse-brasses and artfully-lit 'period' features – you might initially find the decor of the average local somewhat disappointing. You will see ordinary chairs and tables, a nondescript patterned carpet, prosaic curtains and a mish-mash of pictures, prints and objects scattered about the walls and shelves by way of decoration.

These decorative items will sometimes be related to the name of the pub – you may find ships in bottles and seascape paintings in The Navy Arms, hunting prints in The Horse and Hounds, cricket paraphernalia and sepia photos of long-dead cricket players in The Cricketers Arms. Many pub names, however, do not provide the publican with an obvious decorative theme – what would you put in The New Inn? Often, the publican may wisely choose to ignore the name: you are

**Advice:** Do not be put off by the local pub's lack of picturesque quaintness or 'olde worlde' charm. This is the real world. People do not come to this pub to say "ooh" and "aah" and take photographs, but because it is an integral part of their normal social existence.

unlikely to see paintings or sculptures of red lions in The Red Lion, for example.

**Customers**  All ages, types and social classes – the population of the local is as varied as the inhabitants of the surrounding area.

**Behaviour**  Usually very relaxed, friendly and sociable. The local pub is where the natives meet and talk, exchange news and jokes and gossip, argue and debate, celebrate and commiserate. Although the prevailing atmosphere will be cheerful, you may occasionally hear a few heated words, and perhaps even see a few tears: 'All human life is here'.

**Service style**  Despite the somewhat insular nature of the local, you will probably be made to feel welcome. Even if you fail to read or remember the etiquette advice in this book, the publican and staff in the local are likely to be friendly and helpful.

**Drinks**  Do not try order fancy cocktails or un-British drinks such as iced tea, as local pubs are not familiar with these drinks, even though they may have all the necessary ingredients. Stick to beer, cider, spirits, simple spirits-with-mixer combinations such as gin-and-tonic or vodka-and-coke, or soft drinks, tea and coffee. The choice of wines in most locals will be very limited. See Chapter 1, *The Basics*, and Chapter 6, *What's Yours?* for tips on what to order and how to order it – and how the natives will judge you by your choice of drink.

**Food**  If food is available, it will be the simple, unpretentious fare known as 'pub grub': pies, sausages, sandwiches, maybe roast beef on Sundays, and just about everything will come with chips. Most locals will offer some food, at least at lunchtime, even if it is only sandwiches and filled rolls. Almost all pubs have packets of crisps and nuts somewhere behind the bar.

**Advice:** There is an enormous variety of local pubs. If the first one you find does not suit your tastes, don't give up and retreat back to tourist-land. There may well be another local, on the next street corner, in which you will feel perfectly comfortable.

Remember that the local is not a tourist-trap pub, and the publican and staff will not be used to coping with the usual tourist difficulties such as language problems or unfamiliarity with types and sizes of beer. See Chapter 1, *The Basics*, for tips on how to overcome these problems.

although crisps may not be displayed. If there are no visible signs of food, and you are very hungry, it is still worth asking.

Games   The local is a pub where people spend a lot of time. Some may just pop in for quick drink and a chat, but many natives will while away entire evenings in their local on a regular basis. Social bonding is the main function of the local pub, and pub games play a central role in facilitating friendly interaction. In most locals, you will find several traditional pub games, such as darts, pool and dominoes. See Chapter 8, *Games Pubgoers Play*, for advice on how to join in.

Music   Some locals will have a jukebox; in others, the publican or staff will play tapes or CDs – or you may find a live band. In some very basic locals, there may just be a radio playing. In some, usually the more up-market locals, there may be no music at all. You cannot identify a pub as a local by the music – either the means of playing it or the type of music played. But the type of music can sometimes tell you a bit about the type of customers the pub attracts. Within a particular area there may be one local that is favoured by a younger crowd, where you will hear louder and more up-to-date music, and another which appeals to an older clientele, where the music may be more nostalgic or 'easy-listening' in style.

## The Family Pub

If you are visiting Britain with young children, these pubs could transform your holiday. Family pubs have been rapidly multiplying ever since the brewers and pub-owning companies discovered that many pubgoers are also parents. Parents, especially mothers, had long been deprived of the joys of regular pub-going, because children were not legally allowed in pubs.

This enforced maternity-leave from the local was clearly damaging to the family unit, not to mention bad for business, and so the 'family' pub was created. The law was changed to allow under-14s (accompanied by an adult) into pubs with suitable facilities until 9pm. The clues below will help you to find these child-friendly pubs – and if you prefer to do your drinking and socialising in a child-free zone, this section will help you to avoid them.

### Where to look

There are two main types of family pub. One is the ordinary local pub that particularly welcomes children, the other is the dedicated or specialist family pub. The local version is to be found, like all locals, in primarily residential areas away from main shopping centres and tourist-traps, or in suburbs, housing estates and villages.

Specialist family pubs are now mushrooming in town centres as well as on the outskirts of towns and in rural areas. There are now many 'roadside' family pubs on major roads (not motorways) across the country. In town centres, family pubs are competing – and often winning – in the same market as chains like McDonald's and Burger King. The out-of-town family pubs are providing healthy competition for other roadside restaurant-chains.

### When to visit

Daytime and early evening.

### What to look for

| | |
|---|---|
| External clues | The specialist family pubs are very easy to identify. They often display large signs or banners saying 'Family Pub', 'Children Welcome' or 'Children's Menu'. The local, community type of family pub is less easy to spot, but there are a few clues that will help you. For a start, any pub with signs advertising its food is worth trying – 'food' pubs are far more likely to welcome children than dedicated 'drinkers' pubs. In suburbs and villages, look for swings, slides, climbing frames, sand-boxes, bouncy castles and other children's paraphernalia in the garden. |
| Decor | Family-friendly locals do not differ much from other local pubs in their appearance, and even the big, specialist family pubs still retain much of the traditional pub decor. Some of the larger specialist pubs, however, now boast children's play facilities and entertainment to rival the most well-equipped nursery. These may include separate play-houses, sometimes the size of large barns, with 'ball pools', video, games, slides and all types of inflatable and squashy toys. Play areas often have padded floors and walls, and are supervised by trained and experienced staff. |

In some family pubs, you can leave your children in these capable hands for an hour or so while you enjoy a drink and some adult company in another part of the pub. These pubs will also have high-chairs, children's menus, baby-changing

**Advice:** Unless there are signs specifically stating that children are welcome, you should ask at the bar if children are allowed in the pub.

facilities and sometimes even child-sized toilets. Yet family pubs are beating even the most famous burger-chains in competitions such as the 'Parent Friendly Restaurant Awards' because they recognise the needs and tastes of adults as well as children. Despite the child-friendly elements, the place is still a pub – with a proper, grown-up bar; chairs and tables made of wood, not plastic; and a sociable atmosphere.

Customers   In the family-friendly local, the customers will be as described in 'The Local' above, although you may see more couples, more women, perhaps slightly fewer single male drinkers and, before 9pm, more children. The clientele of the specialist family pub will, of course, include a much higher proportion of parents and children. These pubs are also very popular with grandparents, and attract many native 'tourists' and day-trippers.

Behaviour   In general, you may find that native parents who choose to take their children to pubs are rather more open-minded, and more friendly, than those who stick to burger-chains. Pubs are about sociability; burger-chains are about burgers. You are more likely to strike up a conversation and make friends with British families in a pub.

Service style   Service in the family local will be much as in all local pubs: friendly and informal. In the specialist family pub, staff will usually be well-trained and attentive. Their approach may lack the cosy familiarity of the local, but they will be more accustomed to coping with children.

Drinks   In addition to the usual range of beers, ciders, spirits, sherries, wine, soft-drinks, tea and coffee, specialist family pubs may offer milk-shakes and other children's favourites. Some even provide bottle-warming facilities for those with small babies.

Food   The family local will usually provide child-sized portions of traditional pub food, as well as basic child-friendly meals such as baked beans on toast. In the larger specialist pubs you will find colourful, illustrated children's menus, offering dinosaur-shaped fish, batman-shaped potato, smiley puddings and everything else a child could wish for. In fact, the specialist family pubs offer a much wider choice of children's food than the fast-food chains. And in the pub, *you* get to eat *real* food.

Games   Specialist family pubs, and very family-oriented local pubs, are less likely to have a pool table, as this is considered a

somewhat 'macho' game, but you may well find other traditional pub games such as darts and dominoes – perhaps even
Scrabble, which can help to keep older children amused.

Music   There may be background music in both local and specialist
family pubs, but it will generally be less noticeable than in
other pub types. A 'Children Welcome' sign certainly does not
mean that you will be subjected to inane jingles and twinkly
nursery rhymes.

# The Student Pub

Many of Britain's most popular tourist-venues are university towns –
Oxford, Cambridge, Bath, Edinburgh, York and Brighton, for example, are
all as famous for their scholarship as for their tourist attractions. In some
cases, the centres of learning and the tourist attractions are one and the
same. In all of these towns, and many others, you will find student pubs.

## Where to look

No more than one mile from the university buildings or halls of residence,
as most students don't have cars. Students are also far more conservative
and predictable in their lifestyle than popular opinion would suggest, and
they rarely stray very far from their familiar home-territory. They tend to
patronise a few designated pubs within a restricted area.

## When to visit

Student pubs will be at their most lively in the evenings and at weekends.
Some student pubs double as lunchtime and early-evening venues for
shoppers and local office-workers, and may not reveal their true character
until after about 8pm. In the summer, student pubs in the prettier university towns may become tourist pubs, although some tend to attract a large
proportion of foreign students. To see the student pub in its 'natural' state,
you need to visit during term-time.

## What to look for

External   From the outside, student pubs tend to look just like any other
clues   town-centre or local pubs. Having located the 'student terri-
tory' in the town you are visiting, you may have to take a look
inside a few pubs to make an accurate identification – unless
you want to track a group of students through the streets to
see which pub they go to.

Decor   Once inside, the true student pub will be fairly easy to identify.
It will be furnished and decorated in much the same manner
as the scruffier type of local, but with the addition of posters

photos, news-sheets, sporting paraphernalia, scarves, flags and other assorted tribal emblems and totems of the student sub-culture.

**Customers**   Student-pub customers will be casually dressed, with no marked distinction between male and female costumes. You will see some young couples in student pubs, but students generally move in packs, mixed-sex groups being the most common formation.

**Behaviour**   Student-pub customers are generally egalitarian, friendly and easy-going (unless you count the odd nervous breakdown around exam time). They enter the pub like children arriving home from school, shedding bags and coats around the place as they call out greetings, scramble for drinks and snacks and flop into chairs where they sprawl, munch and gulp contentedly. They seem to have little need for privacy or personal space, and do not regard their time as particularly precious. You should have no difficulty in making friends among this sociable crowd, although their apparent informality conceals a fairly rigid adherence to some of the rules of pub etiquette. (See Chapter 3, *Making Contact*, and Chapter 5, *It's Your Round*, for further advice.)

**Service style**   There are two main types of service style in student pubs. Where the publican does most of the work behind the bar, he or she will often adopt a somewhat avuncular manner – indulgent, but with a reassuring touch of parental authority. Where bar staff are involved, they will often be students themselves – sometimes the 'natural leaders' among the student tribe, hired by the clever publican who knows they will attract a following. Their service style will be very informal – you will certainly never be called 'sir' or 'madam', and spilt beer or missing lemon-slices will be treated as minor mishaps, not matters requiring grovelling apology.

**Drinks**   Beer is by far the most popular student drink, as it is relatively cheap, thirst-quenching and more satisfying than a small measure of wine or spirits. While circuit-pub customers (see below) almost invariably prefer lager, you will find more bitter-drinkers among the student population, including a number of real-ale connoisseurs. (See Chapter 1, *The Basics* and Chapter 6, *What's Yours?*, for advice on ordering.)

Food   If food is available, it will usually be basic snacks and 'pub grub'. Some student pubs may offer more vegetarian options than normal. Students rarely have budgets to match their healthy appetites, so you can expect generous portions and good value.

Games   Traditional pub games such as pool and darts are very popular with students, and will be found in many student pubs. Students tend to take these games rather less seriously than other regular pubgoers, and you should find it easy to join in. Pub quizzes are somewhat more competitive – knowledge having a slightly higher value among students than hand–eye co-ordination – but these are still friendly occasions. You may also see more recent inventions such as pin-ball machines, quiz machines and other electronic amusements.

Music   Students have varied tastes in music, and their pubs reflect this. Some publicans will simply play the latest sounds, others will play the current 'cult' favourites. Live music is very popular with students, and student pubs will often feature local bands, or even student bands.

## The Estate Pub

This is, strictly, a sub-type of the broad 'local' pub category, but it deserves a section to itself. You will *never* find an estate pub listed in a glossy guidebook. This is a true native habitat, untouched by tourism – in fact, the estate pub is about as far removed from tourist-Britain as you can get.

### Where to look

The estate pub, as its name suggests, is to be found exclusively on housing estates. These are large, purpose-built groups of inexpensive houses on the fringes of towns and cities throughout Britain. Somewhere among these houses, you will find an estate pub.

### When to visit

Evenings and weekends. Like other locals, the estate pub is likely to be deserted during the day, as people are away at work (except in areas of high unemployment, but here there will be very little spare cash for leisure pursuits, and pub-going will generally be a Friday/Saturday night or Sunday lunchtime activity).

### What to look for

External   Estate pubs tend to be functional rather than aesthetically
clues   pleasing. You will not find any pretty, quaint, old-fashioned

estate pubs, for the obvious reason that most estates, and their pubs, were built after World War Two. The estate pub is usually a large building, and decidedly utilitarian in appearance, although it may well be hung about with banners and posters advertising forthcoming events or promotions. Do not be put off by the exterior. If you wanted a glossy-guidebook pub, you would not have come this far.

**Size and layout**  Estate pubs tend to be big, often with two or more spacious bars, as well as a generously-sized function-room and perhaps even a separate games room.

**Decor**  Unless the pub has been recently refurbished, it will have a comfortably shabby, lived-in look. You will probably see worn carpets, scuffed furniture and fittings and other features reminiscent of an ordinary family living-room – rather than the beams-and-fireplace homeliness of more up-market pubs. There will also be some bold, brash elements: brightly coloured posters promoting special events such as darts matches, live music, karaoke nights – and hand-written notices congratulating regular customers on their birthdays or wedding anniversaries.

**Customers**  The inhabitants of the housing estate. Very few strangers, unless there is a special event on that attracts people from other areas, and no 'passing trade' at all. You may well find that many of the customers in the estate pub are related to each other. There will certainly be no tourists, until you arrive.

**Behaviour**  As in the town, suburb and village locals described above, only more so. The close connections between the regulars, and the almost total absence of outsiders, mean that the estate pub will seem even more like a private club than other locals. The regulars' familiarity with each other, however, may work in your favour, as a stranger will often be regarded as an interesting novelty – a welcome distraction from the same old faces – rather than as an intruder. They will almost certainly want to know why you have strayed so far off the tourist-track. The

**Advice:** If you get into conversation with an estate-pub regular, you would be wise to refrain from commenting on the appearance or behaviour of other people in the pub, as you may well be talking to their uncle, cousin or mother-in-law!

best response would be simply to say that someone recommended this pub to you as a friendly place.

**Service style**
As in the other locals described above, service in estate pubs will generally be friendly and welcoming. The service style will never be obsequious or ingratiating – you are more likely to be called "mate" than "sir". In an estate pub, the customer and the staff are considered to be of equal status, and those working behind the bar will not take kindly to being treated like servants. Respect is mutual, so if you want friendly, polite service, remember to smile and say "please" and "thank you" yourself.

**Drinks and food**
As in the other types of local pub described above, avoid asking for elaborate cocktails, and do not expect *haute cuisine*. Food will be honest, simple 'pub grub', usually served in generous portions.

**Games**
Games such as pool and darts are often an important element of estate-pub life. There may be a separate room dedicated to pool-playing, perhaps with more than one pool-table. As with other locals, you may arrive in the middle of an important league match. See Chapter 8, *Games Pubgoers Play*, for advice on appropriate behaviour.

**Music**
You will rarely find an estate pub without music (the no-music trend being confined largely to more up-market 'serious-traditional' pubs). The wide age-range of customers means that publican will generally 'play safe', both in terms of the type of music and the volume – unless you happen to arrive on a Karaoke Night. Karaoke, a pastime imported from Japan which involves exhibiting one's singing talents with the help of backing tapes, is very popular in estate pubs. The singing is usually loud and unskilled, but the atmosphere is lively and good-humoured.

Estate pubs are not to everyone's taste, but visitors with a genuine curiosity about British life and culture will find much to capture their interest. Most tourists do not have the oppor-

**Advice:** Always show respect for your 'hosts'. However fascinating you find the natives and their habitat, remember that they are people, not exhibits. If you want to take photographs, for example, you should ask very politely for permission – as you would in someone's home.

tunity to spend time in the homes of ordinary natives: the estate pub is as close as you will get to a behind-the-scenery perspective on Britain.

# The Circuit Pub

Young people in British cities and larger towns practice an ancient tribal ritual which involves sauntering from pub to pub on a Friday or Saturday night, usually following a well-defined route or sequence of pubs (the 'circuit'), taking just one or two drinks in each pub before moving on to the next. The pubs on this circuit are known as 'circuit' pubs, although you may also hear them referred to as youth pubs, venue pubs, fun pubs or disco pubs.

## Where to look

Town and city centres. The 'circuit' usually consists of just a few streets within a small central area. Look for streets at the centre of larger towns which are brightly lit and contain a generous number of pubs.

## When to visit

Friday and Saturday evenings only, after 8pm. This is when the young natives flood in to the town centre for their weekly parade around the circuit. Some circuit pubs will do very little trade at other times. Many will have a quite different role and atmosphere during the working week, when they may serve as lunchtime and after-work-drinks venues for office workers and shoppers.

## What to look for

External clues  Identifying a circuit pub from the outside can sometimes be tricky. Many circuit pubs have deceptively ordinary facades, with nothing much to distinguish them from other town-centre pubs. On a Friday or Saturday night, however, there will be a few subtle external clues to help you. First, the music will be louder. You may be able to hear it from the street, even when the pub doors are shut.

Second, there may be one or two 'bouncers' (more politely known as 'door staff' or 'door supervisors') standing at the door of the pub. If neither of these clear signs is immediately

**Advice:** You may need to ask around to find out which pubs are 'on the circuit', as a pub even a few yards outside the ritual path will be excluded.

obvious, glance through the windows: a circuit pub will usually be more brightly lit than other types, and by 9 or 9.30 pm on a Friday or Saturday, it will be very busy. The most popular circuit pubs will be packed with crowds of young people by this time.

**Size and layout**  Again, many circuit pubs are not easily distinguished from ordinary town-centre pubs, although circuit pubs tend to be fairly large, and usually open-plan. There may be two separate bars in some of the very big circuit pubs, but you will rarely find the old-fashioned 'public bar' and 'lounge bar' distinction. The most common layout is one large, open-plan bar – sometimes even with a dance-floor.

**Decor**  You will often notice a lack of cosiness and privacy in the decor of a circuit pub. Young people come to the circuit pub to see and be seen, so bright lights, open spaces and 'posing platforms' – raised areas where the trend-setters can be even more visible – are essential. In the dedicated circuit pub, you will see none of the dark wood, soft textures and comfortable shabbiness of more traditional pub-types. Surfaces will be hard and shiny, furnishings will either be new-looking and carefully matched, or clashing and mismatched in a highly contrived and clearly deliberate manner. Style always takes precedence over comfort.

A theme of some sort may be evident in the decorative features, such as, for example, '1950s Americana', with drugstore jukeboxes, lots of chrome, tail-fin cars, etc. Themes go in and out of fashion very rapidly, and circuit pubs are re-furbished at least twice as frequently as any other pub-type, to keep up with the fashion-conscious British youngsters. The current fads are for 'Sports-bars' with banks of video screen showing satellite and cable sports events, and 'Cyber-pubs' with computers connected to the Internet. By the time you read this book, these may already be old hat, and a new gimmick may be sweeping the youth-pubs of Britain.

**Customers**  You will see very few customers over the age of 30. On a Friday or Saturday night, almost all of the customers in the circuit

> **Warning:** The quiet, pretty, town-centre 'tourist' pub you discovered at lunchtime may lead a double life, becoming a vibrant, crowded, noisy circuit pub at night.

pub will be in the 18–25 age group. You may spot a few stray thirty-somethings, joining in the fun with determined cheerfulness, but the rare forty-something is probably a sociologist writing a book on youth-culture.

Circuit-pub customers are of about the same age as student-pub customers, and have the same capacity to consume large quantities of beer, but there the similarities end. In the circuit pub, customers will be dressed in the latest street-fashions and will clearly have invested some time and effort in their appearance. Females in particular will be much more glamorous than their student-pub counterparts. This is also one of the few pub-types in which you will consistently find equal numbers of males and females – and you will see more large single-sex groups in the circuit pub than in any other type of pub.

Behaviour  Apart from the basic good-humour which characterises all pub behaviour, the comportment of circuit-pub customers bears little resemblance to that of ordinary pubgoers. Circuit-pub behaviour is a curious mixture of spontaneous exuberance and self-conscious posing. The object is to have fun, but also to be noticed.

You will notice that circuit-pub customers, unlike those in the cosy local, are always on the move. There will be a constant flow of customers in and out of the pub, as they consume the statutory one or two drinks before circuit etiquette requires them to move on to the next pub, all entrances and departures being performed with maximum noise and fanfare.

Service style  Do not expect leisurely chats with the bar staff in circuit pubs – particularly on busy Friday and Saturday nights. Service will usually be fast, efficient and cheerful – sometimes even flamboyant – but has none of the cosy familiarity of the local.

Drinks  Fashions in drinks change even more often than the decor in youth pubs. Generally, there will be a wide range of standard lagers and imported bottled lagers, but do not expect much choice of bitters, or any traditional cask-conditioned ales. The current trend is to drink bottled lagers from the bottle, and in some youth-pub circles, asking for a glass will seriously damage your street-cred.

The usual spirits-with-mixers are common, but you may also be faced with a bewildering variety of bottled 'designer' concoctions. There is little point in listing the current fads, as

they will be out of favour by next week, but be warned tha
they are often very strong.

Food　The circuit pub is unlikely to serve food in the evenings
Come nightfall, these pubs are dedicated to drinking, laughing and showing-off.

Games　You are unlikely to find any traditional pub games on the
circuit, although a few youth pubs may have pool tables. You
may, however, see a few pin-ball machines, and perhaps 'gim-
micky' novelties such as table-football, video games or the
Internet.

Music　Usually loud. Music is very important to young natives. The
volume suggests that it is considerably more important than
conversation, which tends to be limited either to monosyl-
labic shouted exchanges or a rather awkward kind of sema-
phore.

If you are invited to join a circuit-drinking group, and you have plenty o
youthful energy and stamina, accept. It should be an experience to remem
ber.

## Variations

Within these basic categories, there are many variations. The 'local', fo
example, is a very broad category, encompassing many very different type
and styles of pub, which include the basic spit-and-sawdust boozer, the
serious-traditional pub and the suburban-stockbroker pub. Some town
centre pubs, although not situated in residential areas, may serve as 'locals
for office-workers, market-stall vendors, labourers, executives and other
who work nearby. If business contacts say "I'll take you to our local", the
usually mean their work-local, not their home-local. If you find a town
centre pub with a particularly friendly, informal atmosphere, where man
of the customers appear to be on familiar terms with the bar staff and each
other, you may have stumbled on a 'work-local'.

**Warning:** Pubs can change type according to the time of day. The work-local
catering to nearby businesses may be full of subdued suited executives at
lunchtime and in the early evening, but become a noisy circuit pub or even
a student pub after 7pm. The family local is another chameleon, where the
atmosphere is bright and primary-coloured during the child-friendly daylight
hours, but takes on the more subtle shades of an ordinary grown-up local in
the evening.

## The classless society

Although the above categorisation of pub-types has inevitably emphasised the social differences between different styles of pub and their clientele, it is important to remember that the British pub is, in general, a 'classless society'. Although some pubs cater largely to a particular social group, you will find a wide cross-section of the British population in most pubs. The composition of the pub-football teams in an Oxford local provides a graphic example: regular players include a head of a University department, a bricklayer, two solicitors, a postman, a financial consultant, two self-employed builders, a biochemist, a maths teacher, a factory worker, a computer programmer, a salesman, three unemployed, an accountant, a roofer, a tiler, a town-planner, a shop assistant – and Joe McCann, MCM's Research Manager and the principal researcher for this book!

# 3

# *Making Contact*

When it comes to making contact with the natives, you will begin to see the advantages of the apparently irrational elements of pub etiquette. You will realise that all these complicated unspoken rules are designed to facilitate communication and sociability.

We have already mentioned the sociable consequences of the no-waiter-service rule and the friendly nature of other practices such as the *"and one for yourself"* ritual. But these are by no means the only opportunities for amicable contact: every rule of pub etiquette has a social benefit.

## Who's who

To make friends with the natives and enjoy pub life, you need a basic understanding of the social composition of the pub tribe. To the uninitiated tourist, the people in the pub are just a blur of faces – we need to adjust the focus so that you can distinguish between different groups and identify key members of the tribe.

### The chief

The publican (who may also be referred to as the licensee, the landlord or landlady, the guv'nor or the host) is the head of the tribe, the high priest, the leader. The skills and personality of the publican influence every aspect of pub life. Even if you never meet the publican, the atmosphere of the pub will tell you a great deal about his or her personal style. The publican is not, however, a dictator. The respect and loyalty of the tribe do not come automatically with the licence to sell drinks, but must be earned. Good publicans are expert psychologists and diplomats, maintaining a delicate balance of friendly sociability and calm authority in all their relations with customers and staff.

### How to spot the publican

Dress   Publicans do not come conveniently labelled. In many pubs the publican will be dressed in much the same manner as the staff, and will be seen performing exactly the same tasks - serving behind the bar, collecting glasses, emptying ashtrays etc. In pubs where the bar staff wear a uniform, the publican may be dressed differently, but in most pubs you will have to rely on more subtle clues.

**Customers' behaviour**

First, watch the behaviour of other customers. Regulars will almost always greet the publican when they enter the pub. The publican is likely to be the person behind the bar whom everybody seems to know. These factors could apply equally, however, to a popular member of bar staff, so when you have identified a likely publican, you will need to observe his or her behaviour more closely.

**Social roles**

Both the staff and the publican will be seen moving around the pub, exchanging a few friendly words with customers while collecting glasses and wiping tables. But the publican is likely to stop for longer conversations with customers during this process than the bar staff. This is not because publicans are lazy or easily distracted from their duties, but because this is an important part of their role. The publican is the 'host', and a good host must do more than keep his or her guests supplied with food and drink. You will notice that a good publican does not show favouritism by spending excessive time with one customer or group, but gives all the regulars more or less equal shares of his or her attention. Watch carefully, and you will see that while the publican chats amicably with the customers, he or she frequently glances around the pub, keeping an eye on who is coming in the door, noting what is happening at the bar or in a secluded corner.

Skilled and experienced bar staff may also exhibit some of these behaviours. In some pubs, you may even observe that the bar staff tend to adopt the mannerisms of the publican – unconsciously copying his or her characteristic posture, gestures and turn of phrase. This is often a sign of a very good publican, but can make the process of identification more difficult!

**Status signals**

If you are in doubt, watch for the person who appears to have no difficulty in commanding the attention of staff and customers. The publican generally does not have to raise his or her voice to attract attention, and a quiet word, or even a look or gesture, will elicit a quick response from members of staff.

## The tribal elders and warriors

So, the publican is the chief of the pub tribe, and the bar staff fulfil the role of official ministers or representatives. It is not difficult to become a member of the tribe, but the established regulars are more than ordinary tribesmen: they are the elders and warriors. They will therefore be among your most important and valuable native contacts, and you need to be able to identify them.

## How to spot the regulars

Position   In a local pub, established regulars will usually be sitting or standing at the bar counter, or seated at tables near to the bar. Unless they have a particularly private matter to discuss, regulars generally like to be at or near the main site of social interaction. They will chose positions close to the bar, from which they can communicate easily with other key members of the tribe. In some locals, certain regulars may sit at the same table or on the same bar-stool every night. If a person frowns at you for no apparent reason on entering the pub, you may be occupying 'his' seat.

Body   The posture of regulars will be relaxed and comfortable
language   indicating that they feel thoroughly at home in the pub. Couples and groups of regulars will often sit or stand with at least part of their bodies facing outwards into the pub, rather than towards each other.

You may also observe a constant flow of non-verbal communications between regulars in different parts of the pub, often conducted at the same time as verbal conversations with immediate neighbours. Without interrupting the discussion, a regular will lift a glass or a chin in greeting as another regular enters the pub, and perhaps even enquire after the new arrival's health with a thumbs-up sign, head-tilt and raised eyebrows. Offers of drinks are conveyed across the pub by the tipping of an imaginary glass towards the mouth, and everyone keeps in touch with a variety of nods, smiles, winks, waves – as well as a number of obscure signals understood only by the participants.

In a crowd waiting to be served at the bar, the regulars will be those adopting a more relaxed posture, not trying so hard to find the best position or catch the barman's eye. Regulars know that they will be noticed by the publican or bar staff, and do not have to exert themselves to attract attention.

If you see the publican or bar staff pouring a drink for a person and handing it over without any order being given, you know that person is a regular. Bar staff will sometimes start pouring a regular's drink as soon as he or she comes through the door.

Names
: The publican and bar staff all address the regulars by name; regulars address the bar staff, publican and each other by name. In fact, you may notice that names are used rather more often than is strictly necessary, emphasising the familiarity and personal connections between members of the pub tribe.

Nicknames
: You will also hear a lot of nicknames – names which are not real names, such as 'Shorty' or 'Doc' or 'Yorkshire'. (In these examples, the nicknames are clearly based on physical characteristics, profession and county of origin respectively, but be prepared for more obscure nicknames with no obvious source, and for contradictory nicknames, such as a very short person called 'Lofty'.) Anyone addressed by a nickname is almost certainly a regular. Nicknames are another key element of the tribal-bonding process. To call someone by a nickname indicates a much higher degree of intimacy than using their real name. Normally, only family and close friends use nicknames. The frequent use of nicknames between regulars, bar staff and publican gives them a sense of belonging – and gives passing anthropologists a helpful insight into the nature of relationships between members of the pub tribe.

Banter
: If a customer appears to be rude or sarcastic to the bar staff – making remarks such as *"Anytime this year will do"* while waiting to be served, or *"Look at the state of these ashtrays, you slob!"* – and receives similarly insulting comments in return, without any sign of real anger, you can safely conclude that he or she is a regular. This ritual exchange of mock-insults and backchat is common practice between bar staff, publicans and regulars in many pubs, and is again a means of expressing intimacy. (For more examples of verbal rituals, see Chapter 4, *Pub Talk*, Chapter 5, *It's Your Round* and Chapter 7, *The Opposite Sex*.)

## Initiating contact

To initiate contact with these various members of the pub tribe, you need to know the correct etiquette of introduction – the best places and times to strike up a conversation with a regular or publican, and the appropriate forms of address.

☑ **Do** stand or sit at or near the bar. The bar counter of a pub is possibly the only place in Britain where the natives feel comfortable about shedding their natural reserve and engaging in conversation with strangers. This is the most 'public' area of the pub, and people lingering at the bar after they have bought their drinks are likely to be the most approachable. People sitting at tables may find your approach intrusive.

☒ **Don't** try to engage the publican or bar staff in conversation when others are waiting to be served. Also remember that even when the bar is not busy, publicans and staff have other tasks to perform – such as collecting glasses, loading the dishwasher, re-stocking the shelves, etc. – and may not always be free to indulge in lengthy chats.

☑ **Do** make use of traditional rituals. Offer a drink to the publican or member of staff who serves you – using the customary *"and one for yourself"* formula. You can, of course, strike up a conversation with bar staff without buying them a drink, but this friendly gesture will certainly be appreciated. If you have a foreign accent, your use of the correct form of words – indicating an unusual knowledge of pub etiquette – may be a pleasant surprise and instant talking-point.

☒ **Don't** be shy. In local pubs, foreign tourists are a novelty, and the natives are likely to be just as interested in you as you are in them. Regulars may well be bored with seeing the same old faces, and will often welcome a diversion, so do not be afraid to take the initiative in talking to them. (If any native does not want to chat, he or she will soon make this clear by answering in monosyllables or by non-verbal signals such as turning away, avoiding eye-contact, etc.)

☑ **Do** approach lone drinkers rather than couples or groups. But if you are male, avoid approaching lone females (and vice-versa), as this may be misinterpreted. Watch for 'open' body-language. Initiate conversation with regulars who are standing or sitting facing out-wards into the room, perhaps leaning back slightly and looking around them.

## How to introduce yourself

Don't *ever* introduce yourself. The *"Hi, I'm Chuck from Alabama"* approach does not go down well in British pubs. Natives will cringe and squirm with embarrassment at such brashness. If your introduction is accompanied by a beaming smile and outstretched hand, they will probably find an excuse to get away from you as quickly as possible. Sorry, but that's how it is. The

British quite frankly do not want to know your name, or shake your hand – or at least not until a proper degree of mutual interest has been well established (like maybe when you marry their daughter). You will have to adopt a more subtle, less demonstrative approach.

Start with a comment about the weather, or a simple question about the beer, the pub, the town, other pubs in the area, etc. Do not speak too loudly, and keep your tone and manner light and casual rather than serious or intense. The object is to 'drift' gradually into conversation, as though by accident. If the person seems happy to chat with you – giving longish answers, asking questions in return, maintaining eye-contact, etc. – you should still curb any urges to introduce yourself. Instead, offer a drink, but avoid using the word 'buy': say *"Can I get you a drink?"* or *"Can I get you another?"*.

Eventually, there may be an opportunity to exchange names, providing this can be achieved in a casual, unforced manner, although it is best to wait for your new acquaintance to take the initiative. If you come to the end of a long friendly evening without having introduced yourselves, and this makes you very uncomfortable, you may say on parting: *"Nice to meet you, er – oh, I didn't catch your name?"*, as though you have only just noticed the omission. Your companion should then enlighten you, and you may now, at last, introduce yourself: *"I'm Chuck, by the way"*. Yes, this may feel a bit like having the soup at the end of the meal. The subtleties of pub etiquette are an acquired taste.

You will generally find it easier to make contact with the natives in pubs outside the main tourist sites. In a busy tourist-oriented pub, you may enjoy impeccable service, and staff will be accustomed to explaining British beers and helping you to sort out your coins – but you will hardly be a novelty. In an obscure back-street or village local, however, a stray tourist will have considerable rarity-value. Your foreign accent may attract attention and interest, and you may well find that little effort on your part is required, as curious natives initiate contact themselves. In many pubs, asking a few innocent questions about the beer, the pub or the region – or even just asking for directions – will result in a flood of contradictory information and advice.

When you find a pub that you like, try to go back a few times. There is a saying in some very friendly pubs: *"You come here twice, you're a regular"*. Two visits will not, in fact, qualify you for the all social rights and privileges of a long-established regular, but it does indicate a warm and welcoming approach. After a few visits to a friendly local, you may well experience some of the joys of being a regular: you may be welcomed by name, offered your 'usual' drink and included in the general chat and banter. Much of this chat and banter will be conducted in accordance with ancient tribal rituals, which are explained in the next chapter.

**4**

# *Pub-talk*

Pub-talk, the most popular activity in all pubs, is a native dialect with its own distinctive grammar. There are two types of pub-talk. The first type, which we may call 'choreographed pub-talk', may initially sound remarkably like ordinary conversation, but the patient eavesdropper will soon detect recurring patterns and rhythms. The second type, 'coded pub-talk', will be utterly incomprehensible to anyone who is not a regular in that particular pub.

These classifications do not refer to the subject of the conversation, but to the way people talk – the structure of their conversations, the unspoken rules they obey, the special terminology they use. There are very few restrictions on what you can talk about in British pubs: pub etiquette is concerned mainly with the form of your conversation, not the content.

## Choreographed pub-talk

We tend to think of rules and laws as unpleasant things, imposing limits and restrictions on our behaviour, inhibiting our natural spontaneity and creativity. The very word 'etiquette' may evoke an image of stuffy propriety. Yet the unwritten rules governing pub-talk are not restrictive or inhibiting – quite the opposite. Like all other aspects of pub etiquette, they are designed to promote sociability. If anything, they encourage *more* verbal exchanges, *more* communication, than would otherwise occur among the naturally reserved natives.

### The greeting ritual

The greeting procedure mentioned in the last chapter is a good example. When a regular enters the pub, you will often hear a chorus of friendly greetings from other regulars, the publican and bar staff  (*"Evening, Joe"*, *"Alright, Joe?"*, *"Wotcha, Joe"*, *"Usual is it, Joe?"*, etc.). The regular responds to each greeting, usually addressing the greeter by name or nickname (*"Evening, Doc"*, *"Alright, there, Lofty?"*, *"Wotcha, Bill"*, *"Usual, thanks, Pauline"*, etc.). No-one is conscious of obeying a rule or following a formula, yet you will hear the same greeting ritual in every pub in the country.

Pub etiquette does not dictate the actual words to be used in this exchange – and you may hear some inventive and idiosyncratic variations. The words may not even be particularly polite: a regular may be greeted with *"Back again, Joe? – haven't you got a home to go to?"* or *"Ah, just in time to buy your round, Joe!"*.

How to join in
: When you first enter a pub, don't just order a drink – start by saying *"Good evening"* or *"Good morning"* (both are often shortened to *" 'ning"*), with a friendly nod and a smile, to the bar staff and the regulars at the bar counter. For most natives, this will trigger an automatic, reflex greeting-response, even if it is only a nod. Don't worry if the initial response is somewhat reserved. By greeting before ordering, you have communicated friendly intentions. Although this does not make you an 'instant regular', it will be noticed, and your subsequent attempts to initiate contact will be received more favourably.

## The pub-argument

A more complex example of choreographed pub-talk is the pub-argument. You may well hear a lot of arguments in pubs – arguing is the most popular pastime of regular pubgoers – and some may seem to be quite heated. But pub-arguments are not like arguments in the real world. They are conducted in accordance with a strict code of etiquette. This code is based on the First Commandment of Pub Law: "Thou shalt not take things too seriously".

The etiquette of pub-arguments reflects the principles enshrined in the unwritten 'constitution' governing all social interaction in the pub: the constitution prescribes equality, reciprocity, the pursuit of intimacy and a tacit non-aggression pact. Any student of human relations will recognise these principles as the essential foundation of all social bonding, and social bonding is what pub-arguments are all about.

☞ **Rule number one**: The pub-argument is an enjoyable game – no strong views or deeply held convictions are necessary to engage in a lively dispute. Pub regulars will often start an argument about anything, just for the fun of it.

A bored regular will often deliberately spark off an argument by making an outrageous or extreme statement, and then sit back and wait for the inevitable cries of *"Rubbish!"* – or something less polite. The initiator will then hotly defend his assertion (which he secretly knows to be indefensible), and counter-attack by accusing his opponents of stupidity, ignorance or worse. The exchange may continue in this fashion for some time, although the attacks and counter-attacks will often drift away from the original issue, moving on to other contentious subjects and eventually focusing almost entirely on the personal qualities of the participants. You may notice, however, that opponents continue to buy each other drinks throughout the slanging match.

By the end, everyone may have forgotten what the argument was supposed to be about. No-one ever wins, no-one ever surrenders. When participants become bored or tired, the accepted formula for terminating the argument is to finish a sentence with " – and anyway, it's your round". Opponents remain the best of mates, and a good time has been had by all

| How to join in | Do not try to join in arguments taking place at tables: only those which occur at the bar counter are 'public' arguments. Even at the bar counter, watch for the 'open' body-language which signals that others are welcome to participate. Involvement of the bar staff or publican is another sign that the argument is public rather than personal. Body-language and facial expressions are also your best guide to the level of 'seriousness' of the dispute. Heated and even insulting words may be used, but in most pub-arguments the relaxed posture and expressions of the participants reveal the lack of any real hostility. Once you have established that the argument is both public and non-hostile, feel free to add your comments and opinions – but remember that this is a game, and do not expect to be taken seriously. Also remember that round-buying is the most effective non-aggression signal. If you inadvertently cause offence, or find yourself in any trouble, buy a round of drinks for your companions. The phrase "I think it must be my round" should get you out of almost any difficulty. (See Chapter 5, It's Your Round, for an explanation of the magical power of the round-buying ritual) |
|---|---|

## Free-association

Psychoanalysts often use a technique called free-association, which involves asking patients to say whatever comes into their mind in association with a particular word or phrase.

Listen carefully, and you will realise that most pub-talk is also a form of free-association – which may help to explain its socially therapeutic effect. In the pub, the naturally reserved and cautious natives shed their inhibitions, and give voice to whatever passing thought happens to occur to them. You will notice that pub-conversations rarely progress in any kind of logical manner; they do not stick to the point, nor do they reach a conclusion.

Pub-talk moves in a mysterious way – mostly in apparently random sideways leaps. A remark about the weather triggers a prediction as to which

> **Warning:** If you are the sort of person who likes conversations to proceed in an orderly manner, you will find the rambling, haphazard, free-association type of pub-talk very frustrating. But when pubgoers are in free-association mode, attempts to get them to focus on a particular subject for more than a few minutes will probably be fruitless and will certainly make you unpopular.

horse will win the big race at Cheltenham, which triggers an argument about the merits of the National Lottery, which leads to a discussion of the latest political scandal, which provokes some banter about the sexual prowess of one of the regulars involved in the discussion, which is interrupted by another regular demanding assistance with a crossword clue, one element of which leads to a comment about a recent fatal traffic accident in the neighbourhood, which somehow turns into a discussion about the barman's new haircut and so on. There is a vague logic in some of the connections, but most changes of subject are triggered by participants 'free-associating' with a random word or phrase.

| How to join in | Free-association is the easiest form of choreographed pub-talk to join in. Having established that the conversation is 'public' (taking place at the bar counter, open body-language, etc.), you just say whatever happens to come into your head in connection with the current topic of conversation. |

## Pub humour

Jokes, puns, teasing, wit, banter and backchat are all essential ingredients of pub-talk. In fact, you will notice that most pub-talk has an undercurrent of humour, never far below the surface.

Pub humour can sometimes be bold and bawdy, but the stereotype of loud, beer-bellied males exchanging dirty jokes is inaccurate and unfair. Most pub humour is quite subtle – occasionally to the point of obscurity – and some participants have a command of irony that would impress Jane Austen.

☞ **Rule number two**: Be prepared to laugh at yourself, as you will almost certainly be teased.

Like Austen's Mr Bennet, pub regulars are disposed to find the faults and follies of others amusing, rather than distressing. A pompous or boastful person will often be encouraged to expound on his favourite topic (*"Oh, did you really?"*, *"Do tell us about it!"*) purely so that the audience may laugh at his self-importance. If you are inclined to take yourself a bit too seriously, to mention your high-powered job more often than is strictly necessary, or to derive too much enjoyment from the sound of your own

**Advice:** Remember that native pubgoers are masters of irony, and particularly adept at maintaining a straight face while joking and teasing. Do not assume that they mean what they say, or take their words too literally. An apparently serious criticism or compliment about, say, your appearance, personal habits or national character, may well be intended as a joke. Never forget the First Commandment of Pub Law "Thou shalt not take things too seriously".

voice – beware! Any over-obvious attempts to impress the highly egalitarian natives will have the opposite effect.

But if you are teased about your failings, do not be upset or offended. Teasing is a sign that you are liked, in spite of your faults. Among regulars, everyone is subjected to at least some teasing – even the most amiable and popular person will be found to have some quirk or mannerism worth laughing at. If the natives did not like you, they would not tease you, but would simply ignore and avoid you.

How to
join in

As a newcomer, it is best to show that you can laugh at yourself before poking fun at your new acquaintances. You may not be able to match the dry wit and quick repartee of native pubgoers, but as a foreigner, you do have two advantages. First, British pubgoers tend to regard all foreigners as intrinsically funny. If you are prepared to laugh at yourself, all of your apparent disadvantages such as language difficulties, unfamiliarity with native customs, ignorance about British beer, etc., are potential sources of amusement. Second, regulars may well be bored with each other's familiar repertoire of jokes, and will welcome any fresh material you can offer.

## Coded pub-talk

Now that you know the basic rules of etiquette, you will find it easy to participate in the various forms of choreographed pub-talk. Coded pub-talk is a different matter. Even if English is your first language, and you have read this book diligently from cover to cover, you will find some pub conversations utterly incomprehensible.

### Example

A busy Sunday lunchtime in a local pub. A few regulars are standing at the bar, where the publican is serving. Publican places a pint of bitter in front of Regular 1, who hands over money.

> Regular 1 (to Publican): *"Where's meat and two veg, then?"*
> Publican: *"Dunno, mate – should be here by now."*

Regular 2: *"Must be doing a Harry"*

– All laugh –

Regular 1: (to Publican) *"Put one in the wood for him, then – and yourself?"*

Publican: *"I'll have one for Ron, thanks."*

De-coding   To de-code this conversation, you would need to know that the question about *"meat and two veg"* was not a request for a meal, but an enquiry as to the whereabouts of another regular, nicknamed 'Meat-and-two-veg' because of his rather conservative, unadventurous nature (meat and two vegetables being the most boring, standard British meal). You would also need to know that *"doing a Harry"*, in this pub, means 'getting lost', Harry being another regular, known for his absent-mindedness. *"Put one in the wood for him"* is a version of a more common pub-phrase, meaning 'reserve a pint of beer to give him when he arrives'. You may hear *"Put one in for..."* or *"Leave one in for..."* in many pubs, but *"Put one in the wood for..."* is a regional variation, found mainly in parts of Kent.

The phrase *"and yourself"* is a contraction of 'and one for yourself', the standard formula for offering a drink. The *"Ron"* referred to by the Publican, however, is not a person. 'Ron' is short for 'later on'. So, Regular 1 is buying a drink now, to be served to Meat-and-two-veg when he arrives (assuming that Meat-and-two-veg has not, in fact, become as absent-minded as Harry and got lost), and offering the publican a drink, which the publican accepts, but will not consume until later on, when he is less busy. Simple, really.

## Silent coded pub-talk

To confuse you further, some coded pub-talk is conducted almost entirely in sign-language, like the following brief 'conversation' between regulars in a local pub.

Two regulars, male and female, are sitting at a table near the bar, exchanging good-humoured backchat with other regulars standing at the bar counter. Regular 1, standing at the bar, catches the eye of the seated male regular, and nods towards the seated regular's drink and that of his female companion, raising his eyebrows. The seated regular pretends to have a heart-attack. Regular 1 says *"Oh, shut up"*. The other regulars fall about laughing.

De-coding   To decipher this exchange, you would need to know that the regular at the bar is not noted for his generosity, that his sign-language was an offer to buy the seated regulars a round of drinks, and that the pantomime heart-attack was an exaggerated expression of shock at this unprecedented offer. A fairly typical 'conversation', but difficult to de-code unless you are familiar with the characters and reputations involved.

There is no short-cut to deciphering coded pub-talk. Every pub has its own private language of in-jokes, nicknames, phrases and gestures. Like the private languages of other social units such as families, couples, school friends, etc., coded pub-talk emphasises the social bonds between pub regulars, reinforcing their sense of 'belonging'.

Private languages are, by definition, exclusive – but don't take it personally. The natives are not speaking gobbledegook just to confuse innocent tourists and anthropologists: coded pub-talk is designed to be incomprehensible to *all* outsiders, *anyone* who is not a loyal member of that particular pub-tribe. The more time you spend in the pub, the easier it will be to crack the code.

# 5

# *It's Your Round*

You can study the ancient tribal ritual of round-buying in any British pub. Just listen for any of the phrases listed below, and observe the behaviour of the speakers and their companions, while enjoying your beer.

Phrases to listen for

*It's your round.*

*It's my round, what's yours?*

*Whose round is it?*

*It's not my bloody round, I got the last one!*

*I suppose it must be my round again?*

*Ah, just in time to buy your round!*

*Where's Steve (or Jim, Alan, Jack, etc.) – he's never here when it's his round!*

*Get the beers in, then!*

*Joe's a good lad – always buys his round.*

*Don't trust Steve – doesn't buy his round.*

*If it's your round, I'll have a pint.*

*He only drinks halves when it's his round.*

*When did you last buy a round?*

*I don't believe it, Steve's actually buying a round!*

*No, I'll get these – it's my round.*

## What is round-buying?

Round-buying is the reciprocal exchange of drinks. In Britain, as elsewhere, drinking is essentially a social activity. Wherever you come from, you will probably be familiar with a practice similar to round-buying, as drinking involves some form of sharing or reciprocal giving in most societies. This is because in all cultures around the world, the ritual practices and etiquettes associated with drinking are designed to promote friendly social interaction – although the naturally reserved British are perhaps more in need of help in this context than other nations.

Reciprocal drink-giving itself is by no means a uniquely British custom. What is perhaps uniquely British, and often baffling to foreigners, is the immense, almost religious significance attached to this practice in British pubs.

☞ **Rule number one**: To the natives, round-buying is sacred. Not 'buying your round' is more than just a breach of pub etiquette: it is heresy.

**Q.** *That sounds a bit extreme: why is round-buying so important to native pubgoers?*

**A.** Because it prevents bloodshed. Reciprocal gift-giving is the most effective means of preventing aggression between nations, tribes or individuals. In the British pub, it is essential. This is because the inhibited British male is frightened of intimacy, finds it difficult to express friendly interest in other males, and can be somewhat aggressive in his manner. Male pub-talk is often argumentative – we saw in the last chapter that the argument is one of the standard forms of choreographed pub-talk – and round-buying is a highly effective antidote these verbal fisticuffs. Buying your opponent a drink is a sort of symbolic handshake, which proves that you are still mates. As one astute (female) publican observed *"If the men didn't buy each other rounds, they'd be at each other's throats. They can be shouting and swearing, but as long as they are still buying each other drinks, I know I won't have a fight on my hands"*. This is a useful tip for novice pubgoers: if the discussion gets a bit heated, and you need to remind the natives of your friendly, peaceful intentions, buy a round.

Despite its paramount importance to the natives, many tourists are never affected by this aspect of pub etiquette, as they only spend a short time in British pubs, often exclusively in the company of fellow-tourists. Their ignorance of the sacred ritual of round-buying is only a source of irritation to the natives when they cause congestion at the bar counter by paying individually for their drinks. If you want to participate at all in the life and culture of the pub, however, you cannot afford to ignore the rules of round-buying.

## The rules of round-buying

❶ In any group of two or more people, one person buys a 'round' of drinks for the whole group.

❷ This is not an act of altruism. The expectation is that the other member or members of the group will each, in turn, buy a round of drinks.

❸ When each member of the group has bought a round, the whole process begins again with the first member.

❹ If the group is seated away from the bar, the person who buys the round acts as 'waiter'. 'Buying your round' involves not only paying for the drinks, but going to the bar, ordering the drinks and carrying them back to the table.

## Exceptions:

❶ In very large groups, traditional round-buying would be prohibitively expensive. This is usually no excuse for abandoning the sacred ritual, however: what generally happens is that the large group divides into smaller sub-groups, each of which engages in the normal round-buying process. Alternatively, a large group may have a 'whip round', collecting a relatively small sum of money from each individual to put into a 'kitty', which is then used to buy rounds of drinks. In some cases, members of very large groups will agree to purchase drinks individually – you may see this occasionally among students and others on low incomes – but sub-groups and kitties are the more common solutions.

❷ In some social circles, couples are treated as one person in the round-buying ritual, in that only the male is expected to 'buy his round'. This variation is extremely rare among younger pubgoers: if you witness it, you can be almost certain that at least the males involved are over 40.

❸ Women generally have less reverence for the round-buying ritual than men. In mixed-sex groups, they tend to humour their male companions by adhering to prescribed etiquette, but in all-female groups you may see all sorts of strange variations and exceptions to the usual practice. (Sex-differences in round-buying and other aspects of pub etiquette are explained in more detail in Chapter 7, *The Opposite Sex*)

## Do's and Don'ts:

**✗** **Don't** expect strict justice in the round-buying ritual. One person may end up buying two rounds during a 'session', while the other members have only bought one round each. Over several sessions, rough equality is usually achieved, but it is bad manners to appear overly concerned about this.

**✓** **Do** take the initiative. If you are visiting British friends or business contacts, one of your hosts will probably buy the first round, but you should be quick to offer the next. When trying to make new friends among native pubgoers, be the first to offer a round.

☒ **Don't** wait until all your companions' glasses are empty before offering to buy the next round. The correct time to say "It's my round" is when your companions have consumed about three-quarters of their drinks. (Beware: the natives tend to drink quite fast, and may have finished their drinks when you have barely started.) The exception to this rule is at 'last orders', when another round of drinks must be purchased even if everyone's glass is full (see the next chapter for an explanation of this strange custom).

☑ **Do** participate whole-heartedly in the round-buying ritual. Any sign of miserly penny-pinching will be noticed and frowned upon. There is no need to be excessively bountiful – in fact, ostentatious displays of wealth will not impress the egalitarian natives – but you must be seen to play your full part in the ritual.

☒ **Don't** be afraid to refuse a drink. If you cannot keep up with the drinking-pace of your native companions, it is perfectly acceptable to say, "Nothing for me, thanks". If you alternate accepting and declining during the round-buying process, you will consume half the number of drinks, without drawing too much attention to yourself. Avoid making an issue or a moral virtue of your moderate drinking, and never refuse a drink that is clearly offered as a significant 'peace-making' or 'friendship' gesture – you can always ask for a soft-drink, and you don't have to drink all of it.

☞ **Insider tip:** You can acquire a reputation for generosity and good-fellowship by always being among the *earliest* to say "It's my round", rather than waiting until the other members of the group have all bought 'their' rounds and it is quite obviously your turn. You will have to buy 'your' round at some point, and delaying the inevitable will only make you appear reluctant and grudging.

**Research findings:** We observed that, on average, 'initiating' round-buyers (those who regularly buy the first round) spend no more money than 'waiting' round-buyers (those who do not offer a round until later in the session). Yet 'initiating' round-buyers are perceived as friendly and generous, and enjoy great popularity among other regulars, whereas 'waiting' round-buyers are less well-liked, and often regarded as miserly. In fact, far from being out-of-pocket, 'initiating' round-buyers end up materially better off than 'waiting' round-buyers, because their reputation for generosity means that others are inclined to be generous towards them.

Although round-buying is a powerful and important ritual, always remember that you cannot simply 'buy' the friendship of the natives. To be accepted, you must participate fully and fairly in the round-buying process, but your popularity will depend on many other factors. The natives will not judge you by the size of your wallet, but by more important personal qualities such as your sense of humour, your social skills, your style of conversation – and your drinking habits, which are the subject of the next chapter.

# 6

# *What's Yours?*

☞ **Rule number one**: Drinking is never an entirely random activity. Whatever part of the world you come from, you will know that it is not socially acceptable to drink 'just anything', indiscriminately, at any time and in any place.

In all cultures where alcohol is consumed, drinking is hedged about with unwritten rules and social norms regarding who may drink how much of what, when, where, with whom and in what manner. The rules are different in different countries and different social circles, but there are always rules.

In some countries, such as Britain and North America, going to a bar before work in the morning to drink a glass of wine or strong spirits would be unthinkable; in others, such as France and Spain, this is a traditional practice among working people. In many countries, the rules governing the consumption of different types of drink involve complex and subtle distinctions. In France, for example, the *aperitif* must be drunk before the meal, different types of wine are served with different foods, and the *digestif* can only be served after the meal. Among the Vlach Gypsies of Hungary, equally strict rules apply to the drinking of brandy. Brandy may only be consumed in three specific situations: first thing in the morning, in the middle of the night at a funeral and by women prior to a rubbish-scavenging trip.

Naturally, we all regard each other's drinking customs as highly eccentric and peculiar, but we generally obey the unspoken rules of our own drinking etiquette without question. In fact, we are often not even aware that we are obeying a rule: it simply never occurs to a Frenchman to serve a drink classified as a *digestif* before sitting down to eat, and a Vlach Gypsy-woman wouldn't dream of drinking brandy unless rubbish-scavenging were on the day's agenda. Even in societies with less rigid drinking etiquettes, we do not drink beer with our cornflakes at breakfast-time, or serve pina colada cocktails with the meat course at a formal dinner-party.

Of course, you are officially free to drink whatever you like in British pubs, and when a native asks *"What's yours?"* (or *"What can I get you?"*, *"What are you drinking?"*, etc.), you can simply name your favourite beverage. But if you are keen to understand and participate in native customs, you should remember that *"What's yours?"* is a socially loaded question.

☞ **Rule number two**: You are what you drink – and when, where and how you drink it.

From your choice of beverage, the natives will make all sorts of assumptions about your social background, your age, your class, your personality and even your sexual orientation. Although some allowances may be made for foreign ignorance or eccentricity, they will judge you according to the rules of *British* drinking etiquette, not those of your own culture.

Most natives will not be able to explain the British rules with any degree of clarity. Indeed, many a native will deny that there are any rules, insisting that everyone drinks what they like in Britain and that he drinks pints of lager only because it is thirst-quenching and he happens to like the taste (just as teenagers claim that they wear the latest street-fashion item because it is comfortable). You don't have to believe him. The fact is that choice of beverage is rarely a simple matter of personal taste. The unspoken etiquette of beverage choice in British pubs, obeyed, consciously or otherwise, by the majority of pubgoers, includes the following rules:

## When, where, what and how much

The British are essentially a beer- and spirits-drinking culture. The popularity of wine is increasing rapidly, but this trend is not yet evident in the majority of ordinary pubs, which still tend to serve only a limited range of wines.

Drinking alcohol before 11am is generally frowned upon. In some middle-class circles, the morning taboo period ends slightly later – nearer to midday – but for most regular pubgoers the taboo is lifted at 11am, which just happens to be the time at which the pubs open.

Some British industries and companies have recently been infected with the 'new puritanism' imported from America, and their executives make a virtuous point of not drinking alcohol at lunchtime. If you are visiting on business, you may need to watch out for signs of this fad.

Although the pubs open at 11am (noon on Sundays), you will not see many people drinking spirits at this time in the morning. Even in Scotland, only 'serious drinkers' will start on the whisky the minute the pub doors open. Ordinary folk are more likely to drop in for a leisurely pint or a half with their morning newspaper.

### 'Last orders' and 'time'

The etiquette on when and how much to drink is complicated by the ritual practices associated with 'last orders' and closing time. At around 10.50 in the evening (10.20 on Sundays), in all British pubs, you will see or hear one or more of the following:

A loud bell will ring

The lights will flash on and off

The publican or a member of bar staff will shout *"Last orders, please!"* (or *"Last orders, ladies and gentlemen!"* or *"Last orders at the bar now, please!"* or some other variation)

Then you will witness a strange phenomenon. The sound of the bell, the flashing lights or the cry "last orders" has an extraordinary effect on the native pubgoers. You remember the scientist Pavlov's dogs, who became accustomed to hearing a bell ring before being fed, and ended up salivating in anticipation of dinner every time they heard a bell? Well, the natives don't exactly start drooling and frothing at the mouth when they hear the 'last orders' bell, but it does seem to trigger a similar involuntary reflex: the overwhelming urge to buy another drink. Apparently sane people, who have behaving quite normally all evening and have full glasses in front of them, will suddenly rush up to the bar, pushing and shoving in their haste to obtain that final pint. We do this automatically, even when we don't really want another drink.

At 11 o'clock (10.30 on Sundays), the bell rings again (or the lights flash), and the publican may call out *"Time, ladies and gentlemen"*. At this signal, you will notice that the natives immediately slow down their drinking-rate. After the mad rush, they now seem in no hurry at all to consume the drink they were so desperate to procure. Having gulped the previous two pints as quickly as possible, they now sip, slowly and deliberately. This phase of the ritual is called 'drinking-up time'. Legally, it takes 20 minutes to finish the last drink. The natives' instinctive, Pavlovian reaction to the second bell is to try to make it last much longer.

Pavlov, in this case, is the nanny-state. In other countries, adults decide for themselves when it is time to drink up and go home to bed. In Britain, we are deemed incapable of making this sort of difficult grown-up decision, so we have licensing laws to tell us when it is bedtime. The publican, *in loco parentis*, has to enforce these laws, ensuring that we all finish our drinks and leave the pub by twenty-past eleven. The result, not surprisingly, is that we behave like rebellious children – whining, dawdling, complaining, taking forever to finish our last drink, hiding in corners in the hope that we won't be noticed and trying to wheedle the poor publican into letting us stay up late, just this once. The ritual ends with the publican and bar staff moving wearily around the pub, chanting *"Come on now, let's have your glasses, please"*, *"Drink up now – haven't you got homes to go to?"*, until the last recalcitrant stragglers eventually obey.

## Who drinks what

Working-class females have the widest choice of beverages, in terms of social acceptability. Pub etiquette allows them to drink almost anything that takes their fancy – from creamy or sweet liqueurs and cocktails, to the full range of soft-drinks, 'designer-drinks' and beers. The only minor restriction is on the size of glass from which they may drink their chosen beer. In many working-class circles, drinking 'pints' is considered unfeminine and unladylike, so the majority of women in this social category drink 'halves'.

Next in order of freedom of choice are middle/upper-class females. They are somewhat more constrained, in that the more sickly-sweet liqueurs and cocktails are regarded as rather vulgar by this social group, and to order a Babycham or a creamy chocolate liqueur would raise a few eyebrows. Female pint-drinking, however, is now acceptable, particularly among students, the under-25s and the aristocracy. Among students, our researchers found that females often felt they had to provide an explanation if they ordered a half rather than a pint. Middle/upper-class females can also partake freely of all wines, spirits, ciders, sherries and soft-drinks.

Lower on the freedom-scale are middle/upper-class males, whose choice is far more restricted than that of their female peers. In the pub, they may drink only beer, spirits (with or without mixers), wine (dry, not sweet) and soft-drinks. Sweet or creamy beverages and fanciful cocktails are regarded as suspiciously 'feminine', and ordering them will cast doubt on your masculinity.

Finally, the working class males, who have very little choice at all. They can drink only beer or spirits – everything else being effeminate. Among older working-class males, even mixers may be frowned upon, gin-and-tonic being a possible exception. Younger males in this socio-economic group have slightly more freedom: among the under-25s, vodka-and-Coke is acceptable, for example, and etiquette allows young males to consume the latest novelties and 'designer' bottled drinks, providing they have a reasonably high alcohol content. But as a rule-of-thumb, you would be wise to assume that anything other than beer or straight spirits is likely to be seen as a 'girly' choice. If you want to drink soft-drinks, say that you are driving or invent some rare tropical disease.

In general, males of the older generations tend to drink bitter, while younger males prefer lager. This is a hangover from the old days when lager was considered a 'ladies' drink' – days which the younger generation do not remember. There are, however, many exceptions to this rule. The Campaign for Real Ale has a youthful membership, and many younger middle-class males drink bitter, which is enjoying a revival in popularity. Among working-class males under 25, however, lager still seems to be the favoured beverage. Although lager has long been accepted as unquestionably 'macho', females still tend to drink more lager than bitter.

### Regional variation: Northern Ireland

In Northern Ireland, the preferred beer is stout (the black stuff with the white top), always ordered by brand-name, usually Guinness. Second to Guinness is lager, with bitter coming a very poor third. The traditional 'Real Ales' are not popular here. The organisers of a three-day Real Ale festival in Belfast claimed that the event was *"a great success"*, boasting that they had run out of beer during the final day. But local drinkers, when we asked for their comments, pointed out that the beer was free. *"People here will drink anything if it's given to them for nothing"* said one cynical pubgoer.

Guinness is also the favoured drink among female pubgoers in Northern Ireland. Of the native female drinkers observed during our research in Belfast, at least 30% were drinking Guinness, compared to about 2% in England. The female pint-drinking trend, however, does not appear to have gained much ground in Northern Ireland, and the majority of females still drink halves – which you will remember are often called 'glasses' in Ireland. One hearty female drinker claimed that her usual order was for two 'glasses' of Guinness – she liked her beer, but could not afford to be seen drinking pints.

**Research findings:** Bar staff in tourist areas told us that Americans tend to be more adventurous than other nationalities in their choice of beverage. They are usually keen to try "real English Ale". A common question from American visitors is *"What do the locals drink around here?"*. One barman said that he usually explained to them that most of the locals drink lager, but that the "historical" English drink is bitter. Another commented that American tourists' insatiable curiosity about British ales can sometimes cause difficulties: *"In an hour, they'll drink a half of every bitter we've got. They don't seem to realise the strength of it. Or they ask for the typical British beer, you give them bitter and then they complain it's too warm – one lady asked for ice in her beer!"*.

### Regional variation: Scotland

In Scotland, a 'wee dram' or a 'nip' – i.e. a shot of whisky – is often drunk alongside a half-pint of beer (a practice which is also common in Ireland). This is a male custom, and you will rarely see a woman indulging in such 'chasers'. If it is so macho, you may ask, why a half-pint rather than a pint? The answer is that 'chasing' each whisky with a half-pint means that you drink more whisky than beer, and as whisky is more alcoholic, this makes you a 'better drinker'. (After several whiskies and half-pints, this explanation will no doubt sound very logical.)

An anthropologist working in the Scottish Highlands provided an amusing example of the male Scots' attitude to what are known in this area as 'ladies' drinks' – i.e. anything other than beer and whisky. In cultures where female drinking is subject to some degree of social disapproval, alcoholic beverages consumed by women are often conveniently granted a sort of honorary 'non-alcoholic' status, such that their consumption does not count as 'drinking'. Among the Scottish Highlanders, this classification of ladies' drinks as 'not really alcohol' is sometimes taken too literally: the researcher recounts an incident in which a drunken man who drove his car off the road one night, miraculously escaping serious injury, insisted that he had not been drinking – he had only had Bacardi-and-Coke!

**Q.** *All this inside information on native drinking etiquette is fascinating, but what are the practical implications for the average tourist? What drink should I order?*

**A.** As a tourist, you have two options:

Option 1　You can take advantage of your 'ignorant foreigner' status and order whatever you like, regardless of the etiquette governing your native companions' choices. This may cause a few raised eyebrows, and among more outspoken natives you may be teased, but you will come to no harm. Your strange drinking habits could even serve as a useful conversation-piece. Don't ask for an expensive drink if the person asking *"What's yours?"* is drinking cost-conscious halves of beer, avoid making derogatory comments about native beverages or drinking habits, be prepared to laugh at your own habits, and you will be fine.

Option 2　If you want to fit in, simply observe the behaviour of whatever group you are with, and copy them. When in doubt, copy the drinking-style of the most popular person in your group. If you find, as many foreigners do, that some male natives drink too much and too fast for your comfort, say so. Express admiration for their ability to 'hold their liquor' and admit that you cannot keep up.

You won't gain much macho status, but your compliment will boost your companions' egos, and, more important, you will be able to remember the name and address of your hotel at the end of the evening.

7

# The Opposite Sex

Some natives will tell you that the British pub is the last bastion of male dominance. They will claim that women can't (or don't, or shouldn't) go into pubs on their own; that the pub is where men go to escape from their wives and children; that pubs are all about male bonding, pints with the lads and so on. You may get the impression that the pub is a macho environment, a male preserve where 'boys will be boys' and girls will be second-class citizens.

Until about 20 years ago, these were statements of fact. Now, they represent either wishful thinking or woeful ignorance. Over a third of the customers you see in the average pub are likely to be female – in circuit 'youth' pubs and student pubs, half the customers may be female – and every year, surveys show that more and more women are becoming regular pubgoers. Publicans are eager to please this growing market, and so pubs are becoming more and more female-friendly. You will still come across a few of the old-style, macho pubs but they are no longer the norm. The pub is no longer a man's world, and would-be dominant males are either muttering gloomily into their beer or busy looking for another bastion.

## Equal but different

So, what's behind these nice egalitarian facts and figures? How do real men and women actually behave in pubs? And what are the rules of etiquette governing their behaviour?

The reality, perhaps surprisingly, is as egalitarian as the research statistics suggest. This does not mean that there are no sex-differences in pub

**Research findings:** Despite some token protests, most native males realise that they have nothing to fear from the increase in female pubgoing. Our research showed that even in pubs with a 60% female clientele, women do not try to take advantage of their majority status. Men were observed to have equal access to the bar stools, dart-board and pool table, and equal 'air time' in conversations. We also found that the male protests tend to come from the older generation: many younger males seem to show a positive *preference* for the more female-friendly pubs – perhaps for the obvious reason that these pubs attract more females.

behaviour. The fundamental laws of pub etiquette apply equally to everyone – but males and females often differ in their observance and interpretation of these laws.

The laws of pub etiquette are designed to promote friendly interaction and social bonding. Any form of behaviour which increases the amount of sociable communication between members of the pub-tribe, or strengthens the social bonds that link them together, is encouraged. All of the rules of pub etiquette are based on five basic principles: equality, reciprocity, the pursuit of intimacy, a tacit non-aggression pact and a prohibition on taking things too seriously.

## Bonding rituals

To the casual observer, the male-bonding rituals and female-bonding rituals that take place in the pub may appear very different, but when you look a bit closer, you realise that both males and females are acting in accordance with the five basic principles of pub etiquette.

Male and female bonding rituals have a number of obvious elements in common. All group-bonding, in any environment, tends to involve a private language of in-jokes, nicknames, catch phrases and customary gestures. These are all in line with the 'pursuit of intimacy' principle of pub etiquette. In pubs, almost all group-bonding also involves drinking – which is conducted in accordance with the principle of reciprocity – although the 'social lubricant' of alcohol is perhaps more essential to the intimacy-avoiding, inhibited male.

The main social activity in almost all pubs is talking, and although music, games and other entertainments facilitate the social-bonding process, it is not surprising that most bonding-rituals, whether male or female, are conversational rituals.

## Male bonding

The most important male-bonding ritual, the argument, has already been mentioned in the chapter on pub-talk. Women participate in pub-arguments, of course, but with considerably less fervour and enthusiasm than their male companions.

Even when they are not actually arguing, men's pub talk tends to be competitive – their joke-telling and word-play often involves a degree of one-upmanship, with participants striving to out-perform each other, or denigrating each other's performance. Among male pubgoers, the need to argue is such that almost any subject, however innocuous, can become a controversial issue. Many male natives seem able to generate a dispute out of thin air. Like desperate auctioneers taking bids from imaginary buyers, they will vehemently object to a statement that nobody has made, or tell a silent companion to shut up. They get away with this because other males are also looking for an excuse to argue. Here is a typical example:

> Male 1: (accusingly): *"What?"*
>
> Male 2: (puzzled): *"I didn't say anything."*
>
> Male 1: *"Yes you did!"*
>
> Male 2: (still bemused): *"No I didn't!"*
>
> Male 1: (belligerent): *"You did, you said it was my round – and it's not my effing round!"*
>
> Male 2: (entering into the spirit of things): *"I didn't bloody say anything, but it is your round!"*
>
> Male 1: *"Bollocks – it's Porky's round!"*
>
> Male 2: *"Then why are you hassling me about it, eh?"*
>
> Male 1: (now thoroughly enjoying himself): *"I'm not – you started it."*
>
> Male 2: (ditto): *"Didn't!"*
>
> Male 1: *"Did!"*
>
> … and so on

This gratuitous fight-picking might appear to be in contravention of the pub-etiquette prescription of intimacy and non-aggression – indeed, you may wonder what all these pointless arguments can possibly have to do with social bonding. The answer is that arguing, for the British male, is a critical element of the 'pursuit of intimacy'. Arguing allows males to show interest in one another; to express emotion; to be demonstrative; to reveal their personal beliefs, attitudes and aspirations, and to discover those of their companions – in other words, to become more intimate, without acknowledging that this is their objective.

Native males have no less need for intimacy than their female counterparts, but they are also frightened of it. The etiquette of pub-arguments conveniently allows them to achieve intimacy under the macho camouflage of competition. The native male also has a tendency to aggression, which pub etiquette channels into harmless 'verbal fisticuffs', using the symbolic

**Advice:** If you want to get closer to your native male companions – to understand their feelings, motivations, attitudes and beliefs – do not attempt a heart-to-heart conversation. Instead, start an argument. If it gets a bit heated, buy a round.

handshake of the round-buying ritual to prevent any escalation into more serious, physical aggression.

Other forms of male bonding include 'girlwatching' (the exchange of proof-of-masculinity comments on the physical attributes of passing females) and pub games (see Chapter 8).

## Female bonding

Male bonding is a traditional feature of pub life. Pubgoers don't usually call it 'male bonding', of course, they tend to use less scientific expressions such as 'pints with the lads'. They are even less likely to speak of 'female bonding', which has only recently become an integral part of pub culture. The female equivalent of 'pints with the lads' is known as a 'girls' night out' or 'girl's night' for short.

Although women have only recently discovered the pub as an ideal environment for social bonding, while men have a long history of 'pints with the lads', female pubgoers have made no attempt to imitate the established rites and rituals of male pubgoers. What women have done is to adapt traditional female-bonding practices to the pub environment.

### Complimenting

There is one female-bonding practice that bears some surface resemblance to the male argument-rituals. Participants in the 'complimenting' ritual do challenge and contradict each other's statements, but that's where the similarity ends. There is no competitiveness, and no one-upmanship – in fact, the exchange could be described as an exercise in one-downmanship.

The subject of this ritual conversation, as with most pub-talk, is immaterial. You will recognise the complimenting ritual by its structure, which is always the same. It starts with one participant paying another participant a compliment. Etiquette requires the recipient of the compliment to respond with a self-deprecating denial, and another compliment in return. This must immediately be countered with a self-critical denial, and a

**Research findings:** Our observation-studies in pubs revealed that women behave very differently when they are in all-female groups. Women in single-sex groups laugh more, talk more, speak louder and gesticulate more extravagantly than those in mixed-sex groups. All of the women we interviewed confirmed that they behaved differently on a girls' night, and over 90% described this difference in terms of a relaxation of restrictions and inhibitions.

further compliment, which is then denied by the recipient, who pays another compliment in return … and so on.

| How to join in | If you are female, it's very easy. Just pay a compliment, ideally followed by a self-critical comparison. Your self-criticism will be challenged, and all you have to do is follow the formula outlined above. If you are male, remember that native males find the complimenting ritual tedious, sickly and utterly incomprehensible, and rarely participate. In older mixed-sex groups, you may compliment females on their appearance, but this is usually done in a humorous, mock-chivalrous tone. As a male, you may never witness the full complimenting ritual: females tend to conduct a more subdued and truncated version of this practice when in the presence of males – or will retreat to the Ladies toilets to indulge in a quick 'round' of compliments. |
|---|---|

## Matching

Eavesdrop on almost any girl's-night group, and you will probably overhear at least one of the traditional phrases used in the 'matching' ritual. To determine whether a girl's group is engaged in this ritual, listen for any of the key phrases listed below.

Key phrases:

*Me too …*

*Oh yes, I know how you feel …*

*Mine's just the same …*

*Oh God, do you get that as well …*

*Really? I do that too …*

*My Mum (sister, friend, boyfriend, aunt, husband, boss, cat, etc.) is just like that …*

*That reminds me of …*

*Oh, that's just like …*

*The same thing happened to me (my Mum, friend, sister, neighbour, hamster, etc.) …*

*I tried that once, and …*

*I can't do that either …*

*Oh, I know what you mean, I'm just the same …*

*So do I …*

*Oh God, yes, I hate those as well …*

**Warning:** Neither male nor female tourists should ever attempt to engage male natives in the matching ritual. Male natives absolutely hate this form of discourse. When they tell you that they were late for work this morning because their bloody car wouldn't start, they do not want to hear that your cousin had a similar problem with her car and was late getting the kids to school. The correct male response would be: "Well, what do you expect if you drive a poncy little Italian car? – I don't get that with my BMW!".

The permutations are endless, but you get the gist. The formula is simple: it is almost exactly the opposite of the male argument / competition rituals. The etiquette of male pub-talk requires participants to contradict each other's statements, challenge each other's views, constantly asserting their individuality and emphasising the differences between them. They achieve intimacy and bonding, and avoid coming to blows, by buying each other drinks – proving that they remain mates despite their differences. In complete contrast, the etiquette of female pub-talk requires participants to avoid opposition and dissent, constantly emphasising the *similarities* between them by 'matching' or 'reinforcing' statements and anecdotes. Female bonding is based on shared experiences and views, and in the matching ritual, participants will go to great lengths to show each other how much they have in common.

How to    When another female tells a story or expresses an opinion, try
join in    to convey – using phrases such as those listed above – that you
            share and empathise with some aspect of her experience,
            feelings or views. (If you violently disagree, or find you have
            nothing in common, do not make this obvious.) If you are
            male, you can join in with the female natives' matching ritual,
            although you will be considered unusual. Make sure you do
            not monopolise the conversation – you will notice that fe-
            males are quite scrupulous about allowing each other equal
            'air-time'.

## Obeying the law

Female-bonding rituals thus look and sound very different from the male versions, but both are entirely in accordance with the traditional laws of pub etiquette. In both cases, equality, intimacy, non-aggression and reci-procity are achieved: they are simply achieved by different means. Male-bonding rituals are competitive and apparently aggressive, but balanced by equal, reciprocal round-buying – and the arguments are a covert means of expressing intimacy. In female-bonding rituals, the pursuit of intimacy is overt, competitive aggression is outlawed, and equality and reciprocity are expressed through allowing each other equal 'air-time' and the reciprocal exchange of compliments.

Both male and female bonding rituals are clearly governed by the First Commandment of pub etiquette: "Thou shalt not take things too seriously". Males manage to argue constantly without actually coming to blows – in fact foreigners are often amazed at the cheerful, good-natured fashion in which native males exchange dire insults. Females manage to discuss each other's problems and traumas without ending up in tears – conversations about divorces and hysterectomies are punctuated with shrieks of laughter, as the girl's-night participants see the funny side of life's disasters.

## Pair-bonding

**Q.** *Is it all single-sex bonding then? You make the native males and females sound like two different species! Are they capable of communicating with each other at all?*

**A.** Yes. We forgot to mention the survey showing that 27% of British couples first met their current partner in a pub! Clearly, the differences in bonding-etiquette are not a serious barrier to interaction between the sexes.

The pub is, in fact, probably the best venue for single people wishing to meet others and make friends. Unlike cinemas, restaurants and other leisure venues, pubs are not couple-oriented. The rules of etiquette, such as no table service and the prescription of sociable interaction at the bar counter, are designed to bring unaccompanied people into friendly conversation with each other.

At the same time, there are none of the sexual pressures and expectations that characterise night-clubs and discotheques. In many pubs, there is a good deal of banter and backchat between males and females. Some of this may be suggestive or even bawdy, but none of it is taken too seriously. By going to a pub on your own, you are not signalling sexual availability, and if you want to sit quietly with your beer, contemplating the universe (or observing the intricacies of pub etiquette) you are perfectly at liberty to do so.

## Tips for solo females

❶ If you are meeting someone at a pub, don't be afraid to go in on your own. You are much safer in the pub, under the protection of the publican or bar staff, than you are hanging around on street corners.

❷ If the pub is full of males who all look up when you come in, don't take it personally. It usually just means that this is a 'local' pub, where people know each other and automatically look up to see who is coming in. An unfamiliar face will, naturally, attract some attention, and perhaps some curiosity, but they will eventually lose interest.

❸ Some pubs are more female-friendly than others. If you are travelling alone, and looking for a particularly safe, welcoming environment, look out for the following female-friendly in-dicators: signs or notices advertising the fact that food is available; any evidence that children are welcome (from ex-plicit signs and notices to swings, slides, etc., in the garden); a friendly smile from the publican/bar staff as you enter the pub; a rack or table of newspapers/magazines.

❹ If you want to be left alone, it is generally best to sit at a table, rather than at the bar counter, as this will signal a desire for privacy. Your privacy is not likely to be invaded, particularly if you make your wishes clear through your body-language (adopting a 'closed' posture, writing postcards, reading a news-paper, etc.). But if you are worried, choose a table reasonably near to the bar, so that you are constantly under the protective eye of the bar staff.

❺ If the bar is not busy, you may choose to stay at the bar counter, talking to the publican or bar staff. If you are engaging the publican or a member of bar staff in lengthy chat, it would be friendly and appropriate to offer him / her a drink.

❻ If you feel a bit 'exposed' when the pub gets more crowded and the bar staff are busy serving other customers, you can always move to a table.

❼ If you are feeling sociable, stay at the bar counter (unless the bar is very busy and you are blocking the path of customers trying to get served), as this is the best place to fall into casual conversation with the natives.

❽ If you accept the offer of a drink from a native (male or female), etiquette requires you to chat with them for at least as long as it takes to consume the drink. So, if you feel at all uncomfortable with someone, do not accept the offer. Do remember, however, that the offer is not, in itself, a sexual invitation (as it is in some 'singles' bars' in other parts of the world) and may be a perfectly innocent, friendly gesture. Your refusal should be firm, but polite.

# Sex differences in round-buying

Among young people, it is generally expected that women will 'buy their round', although males tend to like to buy the first round. If you are female, and you accept the offer of a drink from a male native, it is polite for you to buy the next round. Some older male natives do not expect women to buy rounds, but will not object if you do so.

Others of the older generation simply cannot cope with the idea of women buying them drinks. As a rule-of-thumb, you should always offer to buy your round, but do not persist or make a big issue of it if female drinking-buying is clearly distressing to your companion(s).

**Q.** *All these exceptions and complexities are very interesting, but it's too bloody complicated. I don't want to write a PhD thesis on sex-differences in round-buying, I just want to fit in with the native customs. Isn't there a simple rule I can follow?*

**A.** Yes there is. Whether you are male or female, and whatever the sex or social background of your native companions, the words *"It's my round – what are you having?"* will always be appreciated as a friendly gesture. This line may not be in your phrase book, but it is one of the most useful sentences in the English language.

**Research findings:** Female natives generally don't take round-buying as seriously as the males – indeed, many find male preoccupation with this subject excessive and tedious. We conducted an experiment which involved asking members of round-buying groups "whose round is it next?". The men always knew who had bought the last round, and could often remember up to five or even seven rounds back (which is quite a feat, when you consider that they had consumed a pint at each round!). The women often had no idea whose turn it was, and could not recall with any accuracy which members of the group had bought a round. In mixed-sex groups, females made some token efforts to pay attention to the procedure, but in all-female groups it simply was not an issue. Women do buy each other drinks, but they are not strictly bound by the 'one man, one round' egalitarianism of male round-buying.

# 8

# Games Pubgoers Play

To foreign visitors, some British pubs may seem more like children's playgrounds than adult drinking-places. As one incredulous American tourist remarked *"Look at this place. You've got a dart-board, a bar-billiards table, four different board-games and card-games and dominoes and some weird thing with a wooden box and a bunch of little sticks, and now you tell me this pub also has a football team and a cricket team and on Monday nights there is a quiz! You call this a bar? At home we'd call it a kindergarten!"*

Fortunately for the researcher, this scornful visitor had only noticed about a dozen or so traditional pub games, and had not heard of pubs offering modern novelties such as bungee-running, inflatable sumo wrestling, bar flying and bouncy boxing – not to mention old-fashioned regional eccentricities such as Aunt Sally, wellie-throwing, shove ha'penny, marrow-dangling, conger-cuddling and Wetton Toe Wrestling.

Another baffled visitor asked *"What is it with you British? Why do you have to play all these silly games? Why can't you just go to a bar and have a drink and talk like the rest of the world?"*

The answer is that the rest of the world is not as socially inhibited and inept as the British. We don't find it easy to initiate friendly conversation with strangers, or to develop closer relationships with fellow pubgoers. We need help. We need props. We need excuses to make contact. We need toys and games that get us involved with each other. We need to throw balls and darts together and push little objects around on tables together and keep scores and exclaim over wins and grumble about losses and argue about the rules. OK?

The natives are unlikely to admit to these needs, of course. Instead, they may tell you that it is a historical tradition – that the pub has been the social centre where games have been played for hundreds of years. This is absolutely correct, and sounds much more rational.

Having overcome your bewilderment at the sheer number and variety of pub-games available, and, perhaps, your scorn at the natives' addiction to such childish pursuits, you will probably start wanting to play yourself. To participate, you will need to know the basic etiquette of pub-games. Every pub-game has its rules – not just the rules of the game itself, which would require another whole book, but rules governing the comportment and social interactions of the players.

It would be impossible, or at least tedious, to attempt a comprehensive survey of the etiquettes of each and every pub-game from cribbage to wellie-throwing, with all their myriad regional and local variations. We will cover the basic behaviour-codes governing the most common games – darts, pool and dominoes – and allow you to enjoy discovering the etiquettes of the more obscure games, and regional variations, for yourself.

 **The pub-quiz** is a very popular native pastime. If you go into a pub and see little groups of people huddled, muttering or giggling, over sheets of paper while a 'quiz-master' reads out a series of questions, you have stumbled on a pub-quiz. If you happen to know the answer to a question, ***don't*** shout it out, as you will ruin the game (each team has to write down the answer, and their answer-sheets are then checked by a rival team). Ask at the bar if you can join in the next round.

## Darts

You will find a dart-board in many pubs, as this is one of the most popular pub-games. If you don't immediately see a dart-board, it may be worth looking a bit closer: sometimes the board will be hidden in a sort of cabinet on the wall. If you spot a small double-doored cupboard at about head-height, with a long mat on the floor beneath it and perhaps a chalk-board alongside, you have located the dart-board.

The darts themselves, when no-one is playing, are kept behind the bar, sometimes in a special box, but more often in an old, cracked beer mug. If the dart-board is not already in use, and you wish to play, you must ask at the bar for the darts. There is usually no charge for a game of darts, but in some pubs it is customary to put a few coins in the charity collection-box on the bar counter – and this gesture will always be appreciated.

**Warning:** For almost every common pub-game, there is a 'league', in which teams from different pubs play against each other, all striving to become the champions of their region, or even national champions. You may arrive at the pub in the middle of an important 'league match', in which case it would be highly inappropriate to attempt to join in the game! It is not always easy to tell the difference between a casual game and league match just by looking, but if a number of people other than the players and their immediate companions appear to be taking a great interest in the game, you may have stumbled on a league match. If in doubt, ask.

## 'Chalking'

If there is a game in progress, you must observe the correct etiquette, which is to offer to keep score for the current players. In the language of darts keeping score is called 'chalking', and the correct form of introduction is to say *"Can I chalk?"* or *"Can I chalk for you?"*. The players know that this is not an altruistic gesture, and that your object is to take your turn at the board. Only after you have 'chalked' for the current players will you be allowed to take your turn. If you are not familiar with the game being played, you will have to ask about the scoring procedure, but whatever the game, 'chalking' will require a reasonable level of competence in mental arithmetic.

By 'chalking', you merely gain access to the dart-board when the current game is over. You do not 'join' the game, and if you have no partner you may need to find one. Once your offer to 'chalk' has been accepted, there is no harm in asking the current players if they would like another game but do not be offended by a refusal.

## Sex-differences

Darts is a popular game with both male and female pubgoers. Serious playing – league matches and the like – is always segregated, with separate men's and ladies' teams, but men and women (particularly the younger generation) may often be seen playing casually together.

As a rule-of-thumb, do not attempt to intrude on a single-sex group of darts players if you are of the opposite sex. In some pubs, for example, one evening of the week may be designated 'Ladies' Darts Night', which provides the female regulars with an opportunity to indulge in female bonding rituals.

Males and females also tend to behave differently during the game. Native males generally try to adopt a strong, manly approach, both as players and as spectators. They do not jump about and exclaim over their own or each other's luck or skill. Swearing at one's mistakes, and making mildly sarcastic comments on those of one's companions, is allowed; clapping one's hands in glee upon scoring a double-twenty, and excessive laughter on failing to hit the board at all, is considered 'girly'.

This is perhaps not an unreasonable view, as females – with the exception of serious league players – are indeed given to more spontaneous and expressive reactions, and often have difficulty in maintaining the degree of solemnity required by male players. Whatever the sex of the players, it is customary for the loser to buy the winner a drink.

# Pool and bar-billiards

The dart-board is a more common sight in pubs than the pool table, but this has more to do with the amount of space required for the two games than with their relative popularity. The bar-billiards table is smaller than the pool table, and may often be found in less spacious pubs.

Some purist native pubgoers will object to the lack of proper distinction between pool and bar-billiards in this section. From the average tourist's point of view, however, both games are essentially about hitting balls around a table with long sticks, and there are few differences in the etiquette involved.

## The "Is it ... ?" ritual

Pool and bar-billiards are the easiest pub-games for the lone tourist to join in. The etiquette of introduction is simple, albeit conducted entirely in coded language. All you have to do is to approach one of the players at an opportune moment and ask *"Is it winner stays on?"*. This is understood as an offer to play the winner of the current game. The reply may be *"Yes, names on the board"* or *"Yes, coins down"*. This means that, yes, you may play the winner, and in order to secure your turn you must write your name on the chalk-board near the table or place your coins on the edge of the table. Pool and bar-billiard tables are coin-operated, and it is assumed that you, as the newcomer/challenger, will pay for the game. If the reply to your initial question is simply *"Yes"*, you should ask *"Is it coins down?"* or *"Is it names on the board?"*.

Having secured your match, you can loiter near the table and make further enquiries about the rules of the game – which is advisable as these vary from region to region, and even from pub to pub.

If your knowledge of the game is so limited that you would not even know what questions to ask, try to ascertain the level of skill and/or seriousness (the two are not necessarily related) of the players before attempting to join in. If the players seem very light-hearted in their approach to the game, particularly if their lack of concern is matched by lack of eye-hand co-ordination, you may safely confess your ignorance and ask their advice. Serious, macho players, however inept, may resent the intrusion. As a general rule, bar-billiards players tend to be less serious than pool players.

## "Shot"

Once you have been accepted as a player, you may make appropriate comments on the game in progress. Well, to be honest, there is only one entirely safe and appropriate comment you can make: this is to say *"Shot"* when a player makes a particularly good shot. Perhaps to compensate for the lack of vocabulary, this one word is pronounced in a drawn-out fashion as though it had at least two syllables: "*Sho-ot*". Other players may tease and taunt each other over bad shots, but you would be wise to avoid making any derogatory remarks until you are better acquainted.

> **Q.** *Everyone's seen pool being played, at least in the movies, but most of us tourists have never even heard of bar-billiards: what do I need to know to avoid looking silly at my first game?*
>
> **A.** All you really need to know to avoid ridicule is that the object of bar-billiards is to make the balls go down the holes *without* knocking over the mushroom-shaped objects (called 'pegs'), and that bar-billiards is played entirely from one end of the table. (A group of Scandinavian tourists caused great mirth in a local pub by attempting to take shots from all around the table as though they were playing pool.)

### Quirks and variations

Pool is a more male-dominated game than darts, and you are less likely to find all-female groups of pool-players, although mixed-sex groups are fairly common. As with most pub-games, males tend to take the game more seriously than females and to be less effusive in their reactions. Bar-billiards is more often played purely for fun by both sexes – although males are likely to be more competitive. Some of the more macho type of pool-players do not regard bar-billiards as a serious game at all, and young male natives may treat it as an old-fashioned eccentricity.

You are unlikely to find pool tables in the pretty-postcard tourist oriented pubs, in specialist 'family' pubs or in the more trendy circuit pubs. Search out the back-street locals, student pubs or estate pubs – almost all estate pubs have a pool table. (See Chapter 2 for details on which games are to be found in which pubs, and how to find the type of pub you want.)

## Dominoes

### History

The origins of this game are obscure and disputed, some claiming that it was originally imported to Britain from France, others insisting on a Spanish source, and still others claiming that it came from China, via Italy. (If you get bored with the game itself, which is quite likely, you could always start an argument about its birthplace.)

| | |
|---|---|
| How to join in | The dominoes set is usually kept behind the bar or at the end of the bar counter, so if there is no game already in progress you will have to ask for it. If you don't know the game, and the bar staff are not busy, this could also be a good opportunity |

to ask how it is played – although you may find it more amusing to watch the natives playing and work out the rules for yourself. Either way, the basic game is quite easy to learn. To play it *well* is a different matter, which any aficionado will tell you requires speedy mental arithmetic and great powers of concentration.

It will be difficult for you to 'muscle in' on a game of dominoes, as the winner-stays-on rule does not apply. If you can, try to drift into casual conversation with a friendly group of native domino-players – perhaps when they come up to the bar to buy drinks – and express a keen interest in the game. Dominoes is generally played between friends, so be prepared to take the time to 'make friends' with one or two of the domino-players before attempting to participate. Finding an opportunity to buy a round of drinks for your new acquaintances will help, but do not force yourself on anyone who seems unwilling. (See Chapter 3, *Making Contact*, for further advice.)

If you are lucky enough to be invited to join in a native game of dominoes, and have never played before, you would be wise to watch a few games first, asking one of the players to explain what is happening. The rules are not complicated, but natives tend to play very fast, and you can miss an entire game just by sneezing at the wrong moment. Otherwise, all you need to know is the coded language and the rules of behaviour.

## Language

Dominoes, like all pub-games and most other pub-based activities, has its own special vocabulary. To start with, there are different names for the dominoes themselves, which vary from region to region and from pub to pub. The pieces may be called 'tiles', 'stones', 'bones', 'doms' or, confusingly, 'cards'. The dots on the dominoes are called 'spots'. When you do not have the right dominoes in your 'hand' to fit on either end of the 'line', you do not say so, but rather you signal your inability to take your turn by rapping sharply on the table, once, either with your knuckles or, more commonly, with a domino – this is called 'knocking'.

The game goes on until one player (or, sometimes, two partners) has got rid of all his dominoes. This is called 'chipping out', but the player will just call out, triumphantly or languidly depending on his nature, *"out"*. At the beginning of each new game, as with cards, the dominoes must be shuffled. This must be done by stirring the dominoes around on the table with the flat of your hand, and is, thankfully, called 'shuffling'.

## Behaviour

The vast majority of domino-players are male. This information will immediately tell you much of what you need to know about the expected behaviour. You will be expected to pay attention to the game and not get distracted into idle chit-chat – and you should make your moves without fussing, dithering or otherwise wasting time. Swearing in a manly fashion at your bad luck, or, if you are reasonably well-acquainted, at other players' devious moves, is acceptable; whining is not. Getting angry (*"You bastard!"*) is OK; getting upset (*"It's not fair!"*) is effeminate.

The best players tend to appear very calm and relaxed: in fact, they are too busy counting the spots on the dominoes and working out what everyone else has in their 'hand' to indulge in any histrionics.

Casual domino-playing is usually very good humoured, and each group of players will have its own little rituals, nicknames and private codes. Among one group in a local pub, the players' habit of bemoaning their dreadful 'hands' is parodied in a ritual whereby each player automatically cries *"Oh no!"* in exaggerated mock-horror, as he picks up each of his first 'hand' of dominoes.

By the way, in case you were wondering, the *"weird thing with a wooden box and a bunch of little sticks"* mentioned by the American tourist quoted at the beginning of this chapter is 'cribbage' – a traditional pub-game. It is in fact a card game, played with an ordinary pack of cards. The wooden box (sometimes a board) with holes in the top, and the sticks (called 'pegs'), are only used for keeping score – or, perhaps, to confuse passing anthropologists.

# 9

# Going Native

You now know about as much about pub etiquette as any native regular. The difference is that native regulars have had years of practice, and obey the laws instinctively. It's a bit like the difference between learning a foreign language at school and growing up speaking it as your native tongue. Now that you have read this guide, you may actually have a *better* grasp of the 'grammar' of pub etiquette than the natives, but they still 'speak the language' better than you.

Don't be disheartened. All you need is practice. Everyone knows that the best way to become fluent in a foreign language is through 'total immersion', and, as any of our researchers will tell you, total immersion in the life and culture of the British pub is no great hardship. There is also a long tradition of tourists (and anthropologists) becoming so enchanted by an alien culture that they eventually abandon all attempts at detached observation and 'go native'.

In the context of pubs, you can enjoy most of the experience of being a native without going to the extremes of resigning from your job, deserting your family and taking up permanent residence over here. All you have to do is to become a regular, which is surprisingly easy, and does not require a lengthy stay. Follow the instructions below, and you can soon achieve some of the basics, even if you are only here for a week!

## How to become a regular

First, choose your pub carefully. If you are here in the tourist season, avoid the obviously tourist-oriented pubs and the larger, more impersonal big-chain pub-restaurants. Instead, search out a smallish, friendly local in a back-street, suburb or village. Make sure that it is a pub full of regulars (see Chapter 3 for tips on identifying regulars). Try a few pubs until you find the one with the warmest welcome and the atmosphere that suits you.

Once you have found the right friendly local, demonstrate loyalty by visiting this pub as often as possible – at *least* three times in a week, preferably including at least one weekday evening and one Sunday lunchtime. Going on weekday evenings will show that you are a serious regular pubgoer, not just a casual Saturday-night-out visitor. The pub is also likely to be less busy on weekday evenings, giving you more opportunities to get to know the publican and bar staff. In many locals, Sunday lunchtime is one of the most popular 'sessions' with regulars, when they are at their most genial and relaxed.

At the first opportunity, buy a drink for the publican (or the member of bar staff who serves you), using the *"and one for yourself?"* formula. Also try to find an early opportunity to make friendly contact with the other regulars. Get involved in the chat at the bar counter, and play your full part in the round-buying ritual. If you must order inappropriate drinks, be prepared to be teased about it, and always observe the customary rules of introduction if you wish to participate in pub-games.

### Variations

The precise number of visits required to demonstrate your loyalty will vary from pub to pub. In some very friendly pubs, you may hear the charming old saying *"You come here twice, you're a regular"*. This is not to be taken literally – no-one expects to enjoy all the privileges of a long-standing, established regular after only two visits, but the sentiment is genuine, and admirable. The publicans who use this phrase tend to be those who pride themselves on learning each new customer's name and preferred drink in less than two 'sessions'. Some local pubs may be more insular and wary of strangers, and it may take you a bit longer to gain the confidence of the natives – but achieving this can be an even more rewarding experience.

## The benefits of being a regular

The term 'regular' covers a number of different ranks and positions within the pub-tribe, from the ordinary member to the tribal elder or warrior. But even the most ordinary rank-and-file member of the tribe is a privileged being, and enjoys a sense of importance and belonging that can never be experienced by outsiders. Once you have established yourself as a friendly, loyal, regular customer, you should start to experience at least some of the joys and privileges of this status. These include:

❶ Being greeted by name as you enter the pub or approach the bar. Imagine, after a long day trailing around museums and 'sights' as an anonymous tourist, the sheer warmth and pleasure of that initial chorus of *"Hello, John!"*, *"Evening, John"*, *"Oh, there you are, John – thought you'd fallen in the lake"* – or even *"Ah, just in time to buy your round, John!"*

❷ The publican and bar staff knowing what you drink – saying *"Usual is it, John?"*, or perhaps starting to pour your drink before you even reach the bar counter.

❸ Your very own nickname. If you stay long enough to establish some distinguishing characteristic, or happen to choose a pub where the regulars are particularly addicted to nicknames, you may be given one of your own. The nickname may not be flattering, but when this happens, you know that you belong.

❹ Friends. You may never see your fellow regulars outside the pub – most of them have never been to each other's homes, and would never expect to be invited. But these are friends. The publican, bar staff and regulars in your local are people who take a genuine interest in you, your activities and your concerns.

❺ Information, advice and help. The publican, staff and your fellow regulars are the best source of information and advice on local matters – from where to catch a bus to how to find a better hotel.

❻ The chance to become a warrior. If you succeed in becoming a regular, and show any aptitude for any of the pub-games played in your local, you may be invited to become a member of the pub team. This is a great honour. As a team member, you are more than just an ordinary citizen of the pub-tribe: you are a warrior, going out to do battle for your pub against other tribes. After the battle (known as an away-match) you will return to a hero's welcome, with back-slapping and pints all round. Even in defeat, you will be offered sympathy and sandwiches, and the solidarity of grumbling, excuse-making post-mortems with your fellow warriors.

These are just a few of the many pleasures of being a regular – those which seem to be common to all pubs. In your chosen local, regulars may enjoy all sorts of special rights and privileges that are not mentioned here.

## The responsibilities of being a regular

Along with the many benefits, there are some duties and responsibilities attached to your new position as a full member of the pub-tribe – but don't worry, there are no particularly onerous tasks involved.

❶ You must always greet the publican, bar staff and fellow regulars when you enter the pub – even when you are feeling tired and unsociable. If you have had a very hard day, you may perform a truncated version of the greeting ritual – a few nods and *"'nings"*, rather than everybody's name plus enquiries about their health, etc. – but you cannot avoid the process entirely, however weary or grumpy you may feel.

❷ You must always play your full part in the round-buying ritual. This means always remembering who has bought you a drink, and making sure that you reciprocate as soon as possible; never having to be reminded that it is your round; always being aware of your companions' drinking-pace, so that you can say *"It's my round"* at the correct moment – without, of course, ever giving the impression of being too concerned or calculating about these matters.

❸ You must display a loyal, protective attitude towards your pub and everything and everyone in it. If you become a warrior, you have special responsibility for protecting the pool table, dart-board or other games equipment from any potential harm or damage. You may adopt a somewhat proprietorial manner in this context, preventing 'outsiders' from spilling their drinks on the pool table, for example.

❹ Finally, you must never take advantage of your privileged status. You must not expect to be served 'out-of-turn' at the bar – although this may sometimes happen, simply because a familiar face is more noticeable in a crowd (or because some ignorant tourist ahead of you has offended the bar staff by failing to observe the correct etiquette). You must not monopolise the attention of the publican or bar staff when other customers are waiting to be served – in fact, it is your duty to call out *"Hey, you got customers here, mate!"*, should the publican or staff be engaged in chat and inadvertently neglecting their duties.

In short, being a regular is a bit like being a member of a close-knit extended family, with all the advantages and disadvantages that this entails. The pub, to many natives, is a second home – and some probably spend more time in the pub than they do in their own homes. Most foreigners find it hard to understand the British love-affair with the pub. We hope that this book has explained some of the irresistible attractions of the pub, and, more important, made you want to discover them for yourself.

**Final Warning:** If you go around showing this book to native pubgoers and reading out the rules to them, be prepared for one of the three following reactions:

❶ Some native pubgoers will probably scoff and huff and puff and insist that it's all a load of twaddle (or worse, depending on their vocabulary). They may claim that there are no rules of etiquette, and that their behaviour is totally natural and spontaneous. They are right, in the sense that they obey the laws of pub etiquette without being conscious of doing so – just as we all automatically get dressed in the morning, without reminding ourselves that there is an unspoken rule of etiquette which prohibits going to work in our pyjamas.

❷ Others will not deny the existence of pub-etiquette rules, but will insist that we have got them wrong. They may also be right, in that there are undoubtedly many local variations and exceptions which are not covered in this guide. Alternatively, those who react in this way may simply be trying to start an argument with you, or teasing you, or hoping to convince you that, according to an ancient custom not mentioned in this guide, it is your turn to buy a round.

❸ Finally, you may find a few enlightened individuals who nod and laugh as they flip through the guide, perhaps adding their own insights and examples. These ideal critics might query a few points here and there, but, in accordance with the First Commandment of Pub Etiquette, they will not take anything, including pub etiquette, too seriously!